BECOMING AN UNSTOPPABLE WOMAN

ADRIANA LUNA CARLOS
Editor-In-Chief, Designer and Co-Founder

HANNA OLIVAS
Managing Editor & Co-Founder

ADVERTISING OPPORTUNITIES
Info@SheRisesStudios.com

BAUW MAGAZINE
JANUARY 2026

SHE RISES STUDIOS

CONTACT US
editorial@sherisesstudios.com

WWW.SHERISESSTUDIOS.COM

LETTER FROM THE EDITORS

Dear Readers,

There is something profoundly powerful that happens when women rise together. Not in competition. Not in comparison. But in truth, trust, and shared becoming.

This January edition of Becoming An Unstoppable Woman Magazine is devoted to the momentum that is created when women choose to lead from the inside out and lift one another as they rise. Mentoring Momentum: Women Who Rise Together celebrates the ripple effect of wisdom shared, voices amplified, and courage mirrored back to one another.

Our cover feature, Karen Rudolf, embodies this truth with rare depth and authenticity. Her work reminds us that leadership does not begin with perfection. It begins with presence. With the willingness to listen inwardly. With the courage to honor our lived experiences and allow them to become sources of wisdom rather than wounds.

Karen's story and teachings reflect the heart of this issue. She demonstrates that true mentorship is not about fixing or directing, but about awakening. When women are supported to remember their inner brilliance, they naturally become guides for others. This is how momentum is created. This is how movements are sustained.

As you move through these pages, we invite you to see yourself reflected in the stories shared here. May this edition remind you that you are not alone on your journey, that your voice matters, and that your becoming has the power to inspire another woman to rise.

Together, we rise. And together, we become unstoppable.

With intention and gratitude,

Adriana Luna Carlos, Hanna Olivas
Editors of BAUW Magazine

Become a Managing Partner

she wins
WOMEN'S NETWORK

Join a global Movement of Visionary Women
50+ Chapters. Transformative Community. Unlimited Growth.

WHAT'S INCLUDED

- 40% commission on memberships + event bonuses
- Leadership training, toolkits & ongoing support
- VIP access to retreats, masterminds & more

Join for just

www.shewinswomensnetwork.com

Application Fee (paid only after acceptance)

YOU ARE NOT BROKEN, YOU ARE BECOMING:
THE WORK AND WISDOM OF KAREN RUDOLF

By She Rises Studios Editorial Team

At the heart of Karen Rudolf's work lives a simple yet radical truth: *you are not broken, you are becoming*. It is a belief she did not arrive at through theory or training alone, but through lived experience. Long before she taught it, wrote about it, or guided others through it, Karen had to embody it herself.

There was a defining season in her life when everything familiar seemed to fall apart at once. Her home, her health, her identity, and the outer structures she had relied on began to crumble. At the time, it felt like breaking. Only later did she recognize it as an unraveling, the kind that occurs when life is guiding you back to your truth. Left face to face with herself, Karen learned that healing is not about fixing what is wrong, but about remembering who you are before the world tells you otherwise.

That season became the foundation of her philosophy and her life's work. Each painful experience became a mirror, not reflecting failure, but invitation. In her world of creative problem solving, Karen often references the Japanese art of **Kintsugi**, where broken pottery is repaired with gold. The cracks are not hidden; they are honored, transforming the object into something more beautiful and valuable than before. In the same way, she learned to honor her own cracks, not as flaws, but as places where wisdom and grace could settle. No one, she teaches, is ever truly broken.

When Karen stopped resisting the process and surrendered to it, transformation took on a new meaning. It was no longer about becoming someone new, but about unbecoming everything that was never truly her. From this awareness emerged **The Butterfly Technique**, a method designed to help people pause, shift, and change in moments when life feels overwhelming. It also gave birth to the **Tranquil SOULutions Mind Mosaic™**, a framework that supports clarity when the inner world feels fragmented. These tools were not created from theory, but from lived experience turned into wisdom.

Karen's approach is distinctive because it seamlessly integrates intuition, neuroscience, trauma release, and emotional mastery. For much of her life, she lived in two worlds that seemed to speak different languages. One was deeply intuitive and spiritual, where truth could be felt before words were ever spoken. The other was analytical and grounded in science, shaped by her background in nursing and her curiosity about how the mind works.

Her personal journey forced those worlds to meet. After navigating trauma, loss, and rebuilding, Karen became fascinated by why pain is held not only emotionally, but physically and neurologically. Studying how the brain wires experience, how emotion is stored in the body, and how safety rather than force rewires the nervous system, she discovered that neuroscience and spirituality are not opposites. They are simply different dialects pointing toward the same truth: wholeness.

This integration is embodied in her **Tranquil SOULutions Mind Mosaic™**, which blends intuitive inner listening with the science of neuroplasticity and emotional regulation. For Karen, healing is not linear. It is a dance between evidence and essence, between the science of the brain and the language of the soul. Healing becomes a daily choice, a lifestyle, where one chooses not what happened to them, but who they choose to become.

Another cornerstone of Karen Rudolf's work is her signature **Sassy–Classy–Badassy** framework. Born from her own journey from survival to self-mastery, this philosophy represents three stages of authentic empowerment. *Sassy* is the spark of self-love, courage, and confidence, the moment a woman remembers she matters. *Classy* is the grounded grace of alignment, emotional intelligence, and self-respect. *Badassy* is embodiment, the unapologetic action, boundaries, and resilience that come when worth is no longer negotiated.

Together, these energies guide women out of survival mode and into conscious creation. Survival keeps people reactive and small. The Sassy–Classy–Badassy philosophy reminds women how to reclaim flow, clarity, and purpose. Authentic power, Karen teaches, is not about force, but about alignment. This framework also helped ignite her upcoming solo book, *Spiraling UP: The Light You Command*, which explores growth as an upward spiral rather than a straight line.

Over more than two decades of guiding women and men through subconscious and emotional transformation, Karen has observed consistent patterns. What holds most people back is not lack of talent or opportunity, but the quiet inner dialogue of unworthiness. Many women live in survival mode, prioritizing caretaking, achievement, and peacekeeping over truth and self-connection. These unconscious programs, often inherited generationally, keep women disconnected from intuition and possibility.

Karen's work focuses on bringing these subconscious stories into awareness. Once the story is seen, it can be rewritten. Through processes like **The Butterfly Technique** and the **Tranquil SOULutions Mind Mosaic™**, she supports individuals in shifting from reaction to creation.

When people stop fighting their emotions and begin listening to them, power is reclaimed.

Disruption has been one of Karen's greatest teachers. The personal upheaval that inspired *Spiraling UP: The Light You Command* taught her that breakdowns are not punishments, but interruptions of misalignment. When life dismantles what is familiar, it often clears space for what is true. She reframed disruption as sacred, a spiral that revisits old lessons with new awareness, allowing growth with each turn. Sometimes, she teaches, the fall is the very thing that teaches us how to fly.

Karen Rudolf is a multi-international bestselling author across more than ten collaborative books, including *Sassy, Classy & Badassy*, *Essence of a Woman*, and *Wickedly Smart Women*. Her first solo book, *5 Ways to Create a Ripple*, was self-published as a give-back project, with all proceeds donated and matched to Operation Smile. Publishing taught her that storytelling itself is leadership, a way of giving others permission to see themselves in truth. Visibility, she learned, must always be rooted in integrity rather than image.

That philosophy extends into her role as host of *The Awakening Potential Show*. Holding space for other leaders and visionaries has refined her leadership through deep listening, humility, and presence. Karen views each conversation as sacred, choosing to keep episodes raw and unedited to honor authenticity. Leadership, in her world, is not about standing above others, but standing in service.

In 2026, Karen will also be featured in two documentaries focused on manifestation and healing frequencies. For her, manifestation is not wishful thinking, but frequency alignment. It is about becoming the energy of what you desire through coherence between mind, heart, and soul. Healing and manifestation, she teaches, are inseparable. When internal blocks are cleared, the natural ability to create returns.

Ultimately, Karen Rudolf's work is about reclaiming voice and inner wisdom. Authentic power, she believes, is quiet, grounded, and aligned. It begins when a woman stops abandoning herself to belong. When reflecting on legacy, Karen does not envision monuments or accolades, but ripples. She hopes the women she serves will say she reminded them of who they already were: powerful, whole, and enough.

Her purpose was never to lead the way, but to light it, until others realized the fire was already within them.

Connect With Karen

www.linkedin.com/in/karenrudolf
www.facebook.com/officialkarenrudolf
www.instagram.com/officialkarenrudolf
www.youtube.com/@officialkarenrudolf
www.youtube.com/@AwakeningPotentialshow
www.x.com/karenrudolf

BREATH EXPANSION
THE INVISIBLE FOUNDATION OF STAGE CHARISMA

BY SYLVIA BECKER-HILL

Do you remember that moment you stepped to the microphone—your chest tightening, your mouth suddenly dry, and your own voice echoing back, thinner and higher than usual?

Every woman who has ever spoken from the heart in front of others knows this intimate betrayal of the body.

The truth is: it's not nerves gone rogue—it's breath gone missing.

When the breath collapses, so does presence.

And when it expands, a subtle magic happens: your body remembers safety, your mind slows down, and your voice begins to carry authority without effort. This is the essence of **Breath Expansion**, the first Petal of Stage Charisma™.

The Science Behind Breath & the Diaphragm

Our diaphragm is an elegant dome-shaped muscle—quietly ruling our inner world. When it contracts, it descends, creating negative pressure and drawing life into our lungs; when it relaxes, it lifts, allowing the exhale.

Shallow breathing keeps us locked in the chest and shoulders, a signal to the nervous system that danger is near. Deep, diaphragmatic breathing, by contrast, activates the vagus nerve and shifts us from the stress-driven *fight or flight* mode into calm parasympathetic balance.

Scientific studies show that steady belly breathing increases **heart-rate variability** (the measure of resilience), **lowers cortisol**, and supports emotional regulation and cognitive clarity. In other words, it's biology's oldest and most reliable confidence trick.

Breath Through Time and Culture

Across civilizations, breath has always meant more than air.

THE FRAMEWORK
13 Petals of Stage Charisma™

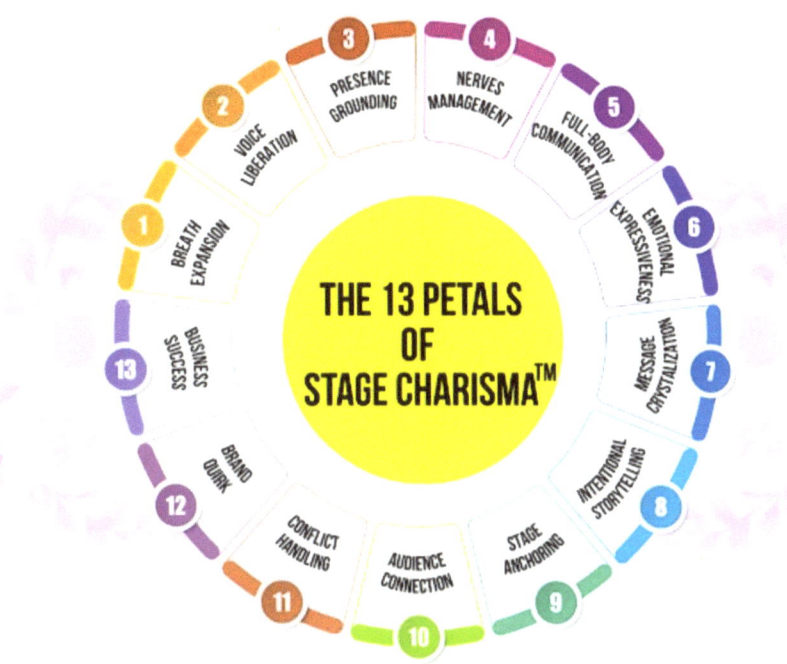

In Sanskrit, *prāṇa* is life force. In Daoist China, *qi* is cosmic energy. In ancient Greece, *pneuma* was both breath and spirit.

Every tradition found its own rhythm to court this invisible power.

Indian **pranayama** teaches how breath can stretch awareness —through controlled retention, gentle resistance, or rapid cleansing bursts like **Kundalini's breath of fire**. In Sufi *dhikr*, breath and mantra weave ecstasy. In Daoist practice, the "microcosmic orbit" guides breath to circulate inner energy.

Whether priest, yogi, or warrior—each learned that control of breath meant mastery of self.

From Breath to Presence: Rodenburg's Three Circles

Modern voice pedagogy mirrors these ancient truths.

The great British acting coach **Patsy Rodenburg** describes **Three Circles of Energy**:
- **Circle 1** pulls inward—nervous, self-conscious.
- **Circle 3** pushes outward—performative, over-forced.
- **Circle 2**, the golden zone, radiates calm authority and real connection.

To stay in that second circle, the breath must be alive, responsive, and generous—never held hostage by fear or effort. That's where charisma begins: in the gentle pulse between inhale and exhale.

The She Speaks LIFE Difference

At **She Speaks LIFE**, Breath Expansion isn't an abstract idea —it's embodied.

Our transformational speaker program guides women through breath-based and body-focused exercises that become daily rituals—strengthening health, confidence, and emotional stability.

Each Petal builds on the next, but Breath Expansion is the root from which all others grow: voice liberation, presence grounding, emotional expressiveness, even business success.

We don't just *teach* how to breathe—we retrain how to *be* breathed by life again.

Because when your breath expands, your story expands.

And when your story expands, the world listens differently.

So, if you feel that quiet stirring in your chest — the one that whispers *it's time to be fully heard* — take a deep breath and say yes to your own expansion.

Scan the QR code to apply for **She Speaks LIFE**, our transformational speaker program where your breath, body, and brilliance become one powerful voice the world will never forget.

Connect With Sylvia

www.becker-hill.com
www.linkedin.com/in/sylviabeckerhill
www.instagram.com/sylviabeckerhill
www.facebook.com/SylviaBeckerHillBiz

Master Public Speaking

SHE SPEAKS *Life*™

Transformational:

- A body that radiates power and poise
- A voice that cuts through noise with truth
- A presence that turns heads without trying
- A message that moves hearts and markets
- The mastery to own any stage, anywhere

Join NOW!

www.sherisesstudios.com/shespeakslife

JANUARY 30, 2026 | 11:00AM– 2:00PM PST

UP YOUR ENERGY
Summit

RISE, LEAD, AND LIGHT UP YOUR LIFE

SHE RISES STUDIOS **FENIX TV**

WHEN LIFE CALLS FOR A REWRITE

By **Candice Suarez**

When I think about some of my favorite things to do in life, I land on socializing around food. It's the small gatherings of friends and family over great food that I imagine most fondly. I love to go out to dinner. I relish in the coffee chats with friends and work connections.

Lucky for me, my career of choice has allowed me to use my gift of gab. I'm an educator by nature and love to speak and present ideas. When I worked in schools, I often found myself doing the morning announcements, leading assemblies, running groups and having lunch chats with groups of kids. As a life coach, I get to conduct workshops, run groups, network and chit chat with colleagues and prospective clients.

Talking and eating. My favorite things.

It's how I find connection. It's how I find joy.

So you can imagine how jarring a diagnosis of tongue cancer was in the winter of 2021. I had just started my life coaching business earlier in the year and had begun college coaching not much before that. Now I was faced with uncertainty.

My biggest and most constant question to my medical team was *"how long?"* I was truly lucky that my prognosis for survival was positive, and I never truly felt my life was in danger. So I wanted to know how long it would take me to speak *"normally"* again. I wanted to know how long it would be before I could eat *"normally"* again. There was a plan. I would make it through this. But what would my life of talking and eating be on the other side of it?

"It depends."

This is a frustrating answer when your two favorite things are on the line. Uncertainty is uncomfortable. It turns out that I could begin speaking again—albeit roughly—within a few days and more easily as time went on. However, my voice is permanently altered. I needed to find the confidence to share out loud (that took quite a bit longer). Eating was a longer struggle. I had a feeding tube inserted into my abdomen for nine months, which allowed me to get the hydration and nutrition I needed through protein shakes. Very, very slowly I learned to swallow again and was able to eat enough food through my mouth to have my tube removed.

Eating and talking now is definitely different. It's funny how things I never had to think about are now strategically planned processes. I don't hesitate to speak whenever and wherever.

I know I can be somewhat difficult to understand, but I roll with it, just much more carefully and slowly.

This whole journey for me is why, more than ever, I connect so powerfully with those in transition. They're in that same space of figuring out who they are in a time of major uncertainty. They are navigating big emotions, unsure of what's ahead, and craving connection. It's that magic space of becoming—not really knowing what is on the other side of this huge, life-changing transition—but knowing that you have to navigate it anyway. You have to move forward.

Helping people find their footing in the midst of change is what I do best. I know what it's like to feel unsure, to lose something essential, and to slowly build a new version of yourself piece by piece. I still love talking and eating, but I also have found other ways to enjoy connection with others. That's what my coaching appoach—*life drafting*—is all about: creating a flexible, evolving version of your life that allows for edits, detours, and growth.

Connect With Candice

www.optimumgrowthcoaching.com
www.facebook.com/OptimumGrowthCoaching
www.instagram.com/optimum.growth.coaching
www.linkedin.com/in/candice-suarez
www.store.bookbaby.com/book/draft-u

DRAFT U

A life drafting journal to self-discovery, goal-setting
& career planning for teens & young adults

Candice Suarez

Illustrated by Olivia Shaughnessy

'REFLECTING, RELEASING, AND BECOMING'

By **Di Kersey**

If I imagine my heart as a box, I can open and examine it. A wooden chest, with the old-fashioned padlock, and a lovely shaped iron key that hangs on the back of the door, out of sight. There are not just papers and photographs within but also scratches on the soft wood on the inside of the lid. Names, scored insults, scarring, points kept, and slights engraved.

There are rejection letters, thank you notes, awards, and missed opportunities.

Photographs of past friends, and long-dead flowers. As I rifle through, I notice the further down into the box I get, the more yellowed and brittle the papers become, as the petals of the flowers around them disintegrate. Photographs have curling edges and age stains, yet a few pieces of paper remain crisp and white, and some of the photographs move like miniature videos. They make me feel hopeful when I touch them. I carefully tease them out so as not to damage the other fragile pieces, and I settle in to read, and watch. I start to smile.

My eyes prick with tears of gratitude, of hope, of recognition, connection, understanding and of knowing, because I hold in my hand the true essence of who I am. Unblemished, presentable, loving, and taken care of, and I remember she's still in there. She remains complete.

The other papers and photographs are crumbling, disintegrating and ageing, and I find they no longer have value or power.

Most of them are almost impossible to read. The writing is so faded, the paper so brittle that some of the older ones turn to dust in my hand. There is a gleam in the corner, and as I carefully excavate my way to it, I notice it is a shiny new gold padlock with a gorgeous little key nestled in its keyhole, and it makes me wonder. Was it here all along? Could I choose the bright shiny thing to gently protect myself, rather than the chunky iron lock that a few struggled to break open, with the key that was not easy to find? As I gently pick my way through the chest, I feel the disintegration in my hands, leaving exposed the shiny white documents, my real self, and I wonder if that was the true necessity of the brown crumbling pages. Have they cushioned the bright white ones and protected them until they were ready to be seen again?

I find myself no longer in need of the dust, so I take out the crisp pages, lay them carefully to the side with the tiny new lock on top of them, pick up the box and shake it out. Taking it outside, I release that dust to the wind, back into the air, back into the world away from me. I return inside and reread the bright, clean pages, and not only smile; I laugh.

The tears are welcome as I rediscover the woman that I am. Putting my tiny lock back on the box, I swallow the key. I'll fill the box every day, every chance I get. I choose what to put in there. I choose what I take within and add to my collection, but mostly I choose those who'll get to wait long enough for me to be able to access the key so that they can help fill the box too.

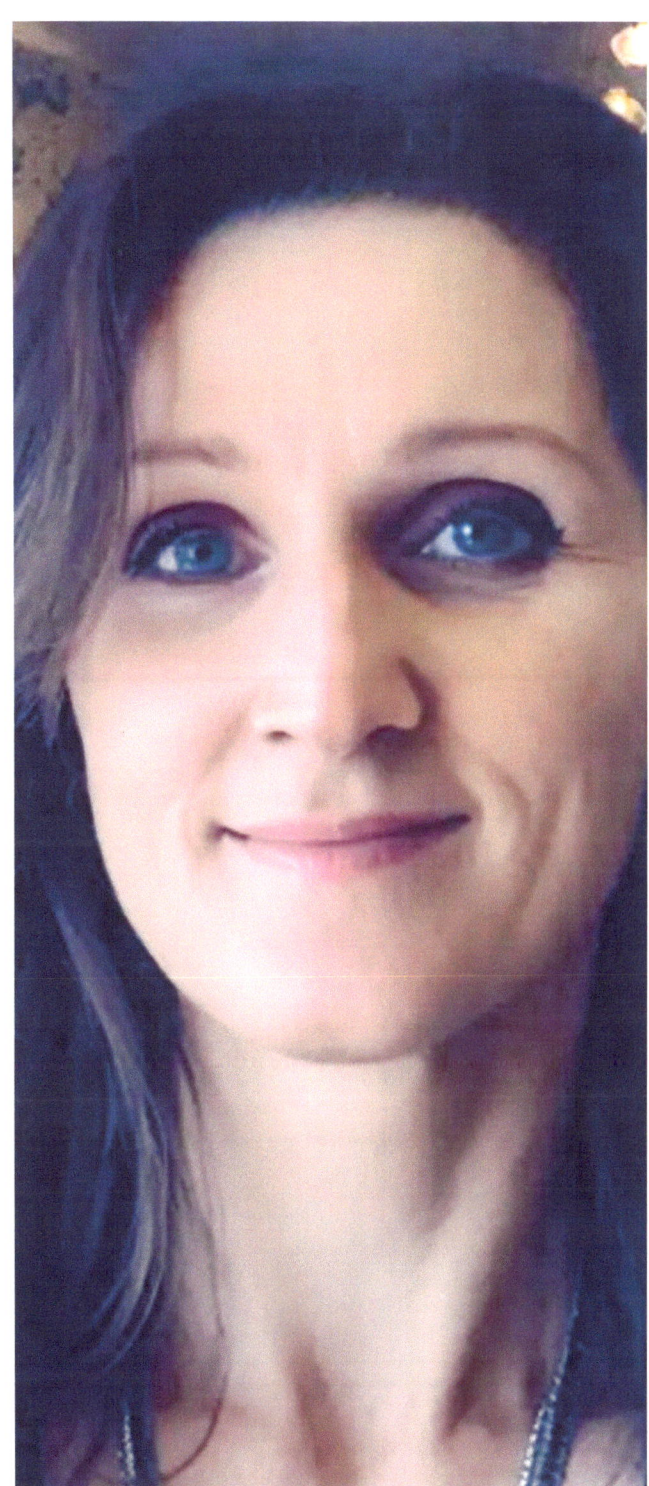

Connect With Di

www.isnteverythingclear.com
www.substack.com/@assumptivewoman?

By **Tetiana Dunaievska**

The year is coming to an end. Everything is changing — goals are being achieved, dreams are coming true, ideas are being realized, and new ones are on the horizon. The world keeps moving forward, but one thing remains unchanged — our ability to receive what we desire through our state of being.

A happy and confident woman knows how to live and feel four essential feminine states:
1. Gratitude
2. Acceptance
3. Relaxation
4. Trust

Today, I want to talk about the first and most powerful one — the state of gratitude.

This feeling creates lightness, femininity, and freedom. It opens the door to abundance — not only in a woman's life but also in the lives of those she loves. The main law of attracting abundance is the feeling of deep gratitude.

What Is the State of Gratitude

Take a moment and think:
What are you grateful to yourself for?

Now, look around — what are you grateful to God, to the Universe, to life itself for?

When we consciously focus on gratitude — with clear, quiet thoughts and no distractions — a pure sense of love and lightness awakens within us. That is the energy of abundance.

It's impossible to be in two states at once. You cannot be in gratitude and in lack at the same time. You cannot love yourself and devalue yourself simultaneously. You cannot live and not live.

You are alive right now.
Acknowledge it.
Pause your thoughts.
And simply feel gratitude.

Notice how your body reacts. Does it feel comfortable being grateful, or is it more used to pressure and self-criticism?

Gratitude as a Path to Abundance

Most often, we feel grateful after something happens. But if you learn to live in gratitude before the results appear, it becomes your natural state of being. Then you start to live in a constant flow of love, inspiration, and inner wealth.

The Universe always listens. It responds not to words, but to your state.

Gratitude is the most powerful law of abundance and the key to receiving what you desire. When you stop being grateful — new ideas, creativity, love, and clarity fade away. It may seem that you haven't done enough this year, that you've scattered your attention on small, meaningless things.

But the moment you stop, refocus on what you have

accomplished, and intentionally bring your awareness to gratitude — something shifts. New energy awakens. Inspiration returns. Strength comes back.

My Personal Experience

I know exactly how it works.

For over twenty years, I have been helping women through coaching to create lives filled with happiness and awareness.

My own journey wasn't easy: divorce, two wars, immigration, losing my business twice, and starting over with two small children. But every time life challenged me, I chose gratitude. I looked within for something solid to hold on to.

Gratitude didn't just help me survive — it helped me be reborn. It brought back strength, inspiration, and love for life and people.

And now I know for sure: if I could do it — so can you.

Invite gratitude into your heart today. Reflect on this year not through self-criticism, but through recognition of how much you have done, created, and overcome.

Let this December become a month of awareness, gratitude, and renewal.

Because everything you are searching for already lives inside you.

Connect With Tetiana

Instagram: @t_dunaevskaya

BRUNCH & BOSS UP™

Brunch & Boss Up™ is not your average talk show—it's a bold, live YouTube experience filmed at high-energy brunch events across the U.S. Designed for the modern entrepreneur, each episode brings together a rotating cast of inspiring business owners, thought leaders, and creatives for real, unfiltered conversations in front of a live audience.

Expect candid stories, fun games, and breakthrough moments—served with mimosas, good food, and great company.

A LIVE BRUNCH SHOW ABOUT REAL ENTREPRENEURS, REAL STORIES, AND BOSS-LEVEL ENERGY

WHERE ELSE CAN YOU SIP MIMOSAS, SHARE STORIES, AND SPARK BREAKTHROUGHS OVER BRUNCH?

Brunch & Boss Up™ is a bold new live YouTube show filmed at high-energy brunch events across the U.S.—where entrepreneurs, creatives, and change-makers come together to eat, laugh, connect, and rise.

Hosted by Hanna Olivas and Adriana Luna Carlos, founders of She Rises Studios and FENIX TV, the show is a natural extension of their mission to empower women globally through storytelling, media, and community. Together, they create spaces where women feel seen, heard, and inspired to lead boldly.

Each episode is filmed in front of a live audience and features a rotating lineup of powerhouse guests who bring their stories, insights, and unfiltered truths to the table. It's where personality meets purpose, and where mimosas meet the mic.

From hilarious games and real conversations to unexpected breakthroughs, Brunch & Boss Up™ is equal parts fun, fierce, and uplifting.

Think Red Table Talk meets UpDating—with a shot of a mimosa and a whole lot of hustle.

Hosted by dynamic duo Hanna Olivas and Adriana Luna Carlos, the show brings their signature energy and heart to every city it touches. Each event is designed to celebrate connection, elevate voices, and create space for meaningful growth and collaboration.

Want to be part of the cast?

We're looking for 4–6 bold, dynamic entrepreneurs in each city to join the show.

As a featured cast member, you'll be:

- On stage, live with our hosts
- Part of the games, challenges, and conversations
- Featured on YouTube and across our social media
- Celebrated for your energy, personality, and story—not just your business

Brunch & Boss Up™ is coming to cities near you.

APPLY TO BE IN THE CAST

Info@SheRisesStudios.com

SLOW, MINDFUL LIVING — ISLAND STYLE:
FINDING RENEWAL THROUGH NATURE, GRATITUDE, AND GENTLE GROWTH

By **Jenna Prieto**
Founder of Mossy Turtle Skincare

"You don't have to chase the light—you are the light."

There's a new kind of glow trending—and it's not the kind that comes from a filter. It's the glow of slowing down, tuning in, and living with deep presence. It's that golden hour radiance—the luminous calm that happens when your mind, body, and spirit are in sync.

As the founder of **Mossy Turtle Skincare**, a reef-safe, island-inspired skincare line rooted in natural beauty, I've learned that true renewal doesn't come from pushing harder—it comes from harmony. From letting your goals breathe, your mind rest, and your heart realign with nature's rhythm.

This season, let the slow living of island time inspire your glow-up. I want to share some rituals for living in tune with an aura that shines from the inside out. Here's how to close out the year with peace, presence, and purpose—so you can step into 2026 radiant, renewed, and unstoppable.

The Golden Hour Gratitude Ritual

Put the phone down. Step into the light. Feel the sun warm your face.

At the end of each day, take five slow breaths and reflect as the sky turns gold. Ask yourself:
- What made me smile today?
- What am I grateful for—even if it wasn't perfect?
- What am I ready to release before tomorrow?

This simple ritual, inspired by the rhythm of the sunset, is your **golden hour detox**. Gratitude is the ultimate glow-up— it softens tension, centers your energy, and brings back your inner light. No serum can replicate that.

"Gratitude is a filter for your energy—it helps you radiate from the inside out."

Gentle Growth Is the New Grind

Busy is out. Balanced is in.

We've been told that growth means more- more doing, more achieving, more pressure. But nature reminds us that even the strongest trees rest in winter. Growth doesn't always mean acceleration; sometimes it means alignment.

Try this: instead of creating a long list of resolutions, choose one word to guide your next chapter- *ease, radiance, abundance,* or *flow.* Let it anchor you when the world speeds up.

When you move through life with intention instead of intensity, you attract peace that lasts- and success that feels aligned.

The Island Glow Renewal Ritual

When it's time to release, reset, and reconnect, this island-inspired ritual brings you back to center.

Your Ritual:
- Fill your bath or shower with steam and a few drops of

your favorite essential oil (mine is amber oil).
- Put on your favorite chill playlist or ocean sounds.
- As you bathe, visualize the water washing away stress, comparison, and any energy that feels heavy.
- Here's your mini staycation- just make sure to enjoy it on island time.

Afterward, apply your favorite reef-safe moisturizer like *Mossy Turtle's Glassy Surf Reef Kind Facial Cream-* and let your skin drink in the hydration. Pair it with a few minutes of red light therapy or gua sha to enhance circulation and boost your outer glow to match your inner peace.
It's not just skincare- it's soul care.

The Glow of Going Slow

When you move slower, you feel more. You see more. You shine more.

Island-style slow living teaches us that slowing down isn't lazy- it's *luxury.* It's where creativity, clarity, and confidence grow.

As you enter 2026, remember: you don't need to chase the light. You already *are* the light.

Here's to your golden hour era—radiant, rested, and unstoppable.

Connect With Jenna

www.MossyTurtleSkincare.com
Instagram: @MossyTurtleSkincare
Tiktok: @MossyTurtleSkincare

FROM LAYOFF TO LAUNCH:
A FIVE-YEAR JOURNEY OF REINVENTION

By **Caitlin Moyer**

When I was laid off from my full-time job in October 2020, it felt like the ground had dropped out from under me. After 18 years with the same organization, what many considered a dream job, I suddenly had nowhere to be on a Tuesday morning. Friends offered well-meaning clichés about doors closing and opening, and I appreciated the sentiment even if I was not quite ready to believe it yet.

I had thought about going out on my own for years, but I was comfortable. I had a steady paycheck, good benefits, and a role people envied. Why would I leave? People would not understand. So I stayed even as the idea of building something of my own kept quietly tugging at me. The layoff did not give me a choice. It gave me permission.

Those first few weeks were disorienting. I went on long runs just to get fresh air and clear my head, which eventually turned into marathon training. I held virtual and socially distanced yoga sessions in my living room or backyard because moving my body and inspiring others to do the same was the only thing that quieted the noise. I journaled to get the spiral out of my head and onto paper, and I practiced meditation whenever I could carve out a few quiet minutes. These were not curated self-care rituals. They were practical ways to survive and regain a sense of control amid the uncertainty.

As the fog lifted, I faced a decision. I could find another full-time desk job, the safe and expected route. But I kept asking myself: if I do not try to build my own thing now, in the middle of a pandemic, will I be sitting at that same desk 20 years from now wondering what if? Desk jobs would always be there if I failed. This moment might not come again.

So I took the leap. I launched Caitlin Moyer Communications & Marketing while simultaneously pursuing personal training and yoga instructor certifications. It felt equal parts exhilarating and terrifying. I was combining nearly two decades of communications and marketing expertise with my passion for fitness and wellness, but on my own terms this time.

The journey was messy. There were months when work was sparse and I second-guessed everything. I studied for certification exams late at night, caffeinated and stressed. Slowly, things started clicking. A client here, a successful class there. Each small win reminded me why I had chosen this path. I learned to trust my instincts, say no to projects that did not feel right, and build a business that actually reflected my values.

Five years later, here is what I know. My only regret is that I did not do this sooner. I have the freedom to create my own schedule, choose the clients and projects I take on, and work with people and brands I actually trust and believe in. My work-life balance is better than it has ever been. I thought I would miss the extensive travel that came with my old role, but instead I am excited to be home, to not miss random summer afternoons, and to travel on my own terms when I want to.

The layoff forced me to do what I had been too comfortable to do myself. It forced me to bet on me. If you are in a role that feels safe but not quite right, or if you have been laid off and are wondering what comes next, here is what I wish I had known sooner. Comfort is expensive. It costs you the chance to find out what you are capable of. You do not need to wait for permission or the perfect moment.

You just need to start. Find practices that keep you grounded when everything feels uncertain. Trust yourself even when it is scary. The leap you are afraid to take might be exactly the one you need.

That layoff did not ruin my career. It freed me to finally build the one I had been too scared to pursue. Five years later, I am running my own business, teaching yoga and personal training, and living life on my terms. If I could go back to that version of me sitting at her kitchen table in October 2020, I would tell her: this is the beginning of something better. Trust yourself. Take the leap. You will not regret it.

Connect With Caitlin

www.CaitlinMoyer.com
Instagram: @CaitlinMoyer
www.linkedin.com/in/caitlinmoyer
www.facebook.com/Caitlin.Moyer
Twitter/X: @CMoyer
TikTok: @CMoyer
YouTube: @CMoyer

FROM BROKEN TO BECOMING:
THE POWER OF SELF-CARE AFTER DIVORCE

By **Ellen Wright, Esq.**

Divorce has a way of stripping life down to its bones. It challenges your identity, your confidence, and your sense of safety. As a divorce and family law attorney, I've guided many women through this transition—but before I ever represented a client, I lived it myself.

As an unwed mother and a woman in long-term recovery from alcoholism, I've sat in that courtroom wondering how I'd rebuild. I know the exhaustion of pretending to be *"fine"* when you're anything but. Yet I've learned this truth: self-care isn't a luxury during divorce—it's a lifeline.

Self-Care as Survival

For women in divorce, self-care can feel impossible. You're too tired, too busy, too heartbroken. But caring for yourself isn't about bubble baths or indulgence—it's about survival. It's the simple, grounding acts that keep you steady when everything else feels uncertain.

Self-care often starts in the quiet moments when you start to zero out the noise. What it looks like for everyone is different, but it can be as simple as choosing calm instead of conflict, fixing something wholesome to eat instead of fast food, or giving yourself permission to rest even when that nagging voice says you haven't done enough. Each mindful decision becomes a small declaration of worth. Over time, these choices add up.

In my 30-Day Divorce Self-Care Challenge, I've watched women rediscover stability and confidence simply by showing up for themselves in small, consistent ways.

Reflection: Meeting Yourself Again

Divorce asks the hardest questions: Who am I now? What do I need? What do I deserve? Reflection is the act of meeting yourself again without judgment or apology.

When I began my own recovery, reflection forced me to face what I'd ignored—how often I'd silenced my needs to keep the peace. The answers weren't easy, but they were freeing. Reflection isn't about reliving pain; it's about reclaiming power. Write your thoughts. Speak them aloud. Sit in stillness until you hear your own voice again. That voice becomes your anchor.

Renewal: Remembering Yourself

Renewal doesn't require reinvention—it requires remembering. It begins when you give yourself permission to heal at your own pace and stop apologizing for taking up space.

True self-care teaches boundaries. You start saying no to chaos and yes to calm. You choose sleep, solitude, or laughter over endless worry. You realize peace doesn't arrive by accident—it's something you build through consistent, gentle choices.

Renewal is also rediscovering joy—the morning you wake up without crying, the first deep breath that doesn't hurt, the small moment that makes you laugh again. Those are milestones of becoming.

Resilience: The Power Within

Women are conditioned to hold everything together—for our families, our children, our work. But real strength isn't about holding on; it's about knowing when to let go. Resilience grows from rest, not resistance.

I've watched women transform before my eyes—the mother who found her voice in court, the professional who rebuilt her career, the survivor who learned to love again. They didn't find strength by forcing it. They found it by caring for themselves long enough to believe they were worth saving.

As the year draws to a close, I encourage every woman navigating divorce to start small. Drink water. Take a walk. Write one kind sentence to yourself. Healing isn't about doing everything; it's about doing something—every single day.

Because self-care is how you rise.
You are not the woman who fell apart.
You are the woman who decided she was worth rebuilding for.

Connect With Ellen

www.youtube.com/@wrightfamilylawgroup
www.instagram.com/wrightfamilylaw
www.facebook.com/WrightFamilyLawGroup
www.tiktok.com/@wrightfamilylawgroup

"Narc Narc, Who's There"   The Memoir They Tried to Silence.

When the mask comes off, the truth screams. "Narc Narc, Who's There" is more than a story; it's evidence. Built from real documents, photos, and lived pain, it shatters the illusion of narcissistic abuse and exposes what really happens behind closed doors.

This is my fight to end the cycle, to protect my daughter Faith, and to prove that love, truth, and resilience are stronger than manipulation and control.
For every survivor who has ever been gaslit or silenced, this is your validation.

Raw. Real. Unforgettable.

Now available on Amazon.

She thought she was preparing for motherhood. Instead, she was preparing to survive him. What should have been the happiest year of her life spiraled into horror, an alcoholic psychopath, a pregnancy in danger, and a desperate fight to stay alive.

He stole her safety. He shattered her body. He almost stole her life. But in the silence of fear, something refused to surrender, her unborn daughter. A true story that pierces the soul, one that lingers, shakes, and refuses to be forgotten.

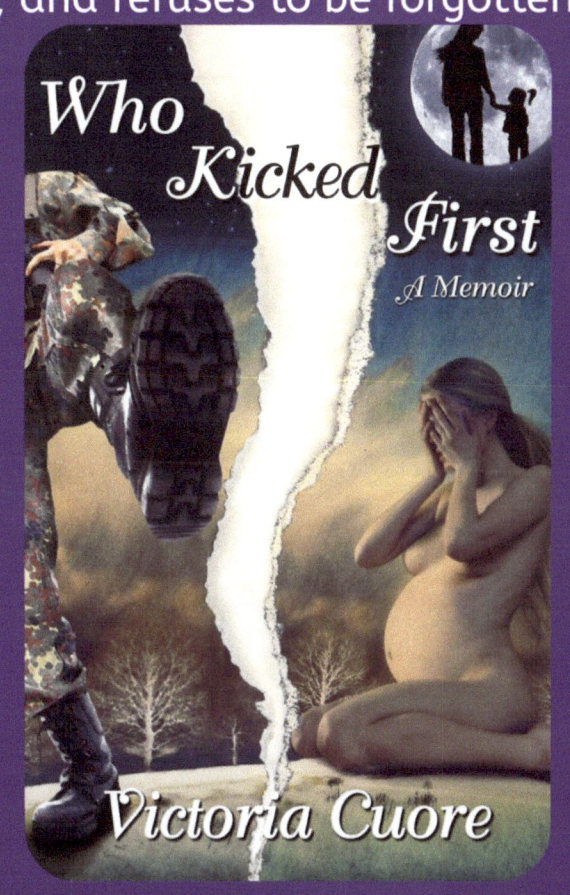

Now available on Amazon.

About Victoria Cuore:

Victoria Cuore is a globally recognized survivor-advocate, amputee, and founder of A Contagious Smile, an award-winning trauma-informed platform changing lives worldwide.
Having endured over a hundred surgeries and unimaginable abuse, she now uses her story to ignite hope and give survivors the one thing she fought hardest to reclaim: their voice.

RECLAIMING THE HEART OF YOUR LEADERSHIP

By **Brianna Sylver**
Founder & President, Sylver Consulting | Author of *"Leading Through Free Fall: How Innovators Turn Turbulence into Trust"*

For years, I believed strong leadership meant carrying everything and everyone. I said yes to every need. I pushed through long days and late nights. I felt useful and important, yet something inside me was growing quiet.

My schedule looked successful. My spirit did not.

The shift began in a season when our company numbers looked great but inside our culture, I sensed strain. Conversations felt tense. Projects lost their spark. I was still delivering outcomes, but I did not like the energy I was bringing into the room. I also didn't love what was being reflected back at me.

The truth was simple: I had drifted away from myself.

Renewal began with reflection. I slowed down and asked hard questions:
What presence do I bring when I enter a meeting?
What habits are running in the background that no one sees?
What do I truly value as a leader and as a human being?

Journaling helped me name what I could not see during the daily rush.

My perfectionism had been posing as dedication.
Overprotection had been limiting my team's growth.
Service without boundaries had turned genuine, generous effort into quiet resentment.
None of this felt like the leader I wanted to be.

With honest reflection came clarity. Three values rose to the surface and now guide my choices every day: Shared appreciation. Collaboration. Personal responsibility.

These values are simple to write and powerful to live. They ask me to notice the good in others. They ask me to design spaces where people participate, not just observe. They ask me to follow through on what I say and to invite my team to do the same.

When I began to lead from this foundation, the tone of our work completely changed. Meetings opened up, feedback felt safer, we reconnected to purpose, and I felt joy return to the craft of building ideas with people I trust.

In my client work, I meet many leaders who carry a similar weight. They are accomplished and exhausted. They look for relief in new frameworks or more data. The turning point often arrives when they pause long enough to ask one simple question. Who am I being right now?

That question brings the human heart of leadership back into view. It reminds us that people remember how we made them feel. It invites us to notice where fear is steering a decision. And it asks us to choose presence over performance.

From that place, trust grows and progress follows closely behind.

Reflection is not a luxury. It is a practical tool for clarity.
It helps us sort urgency from importance and motion from momentum.

It also restores something essential. When I make time to reflect, I remember that leadership begins within me, then extends to others. I show up grounded. I listen better. I ask cleaner questions. I keep my word. Small actions compound into a culture people can rely on.

If you are in a season that feels heavy, try this simple practice:
Take ten minutes with a blank page. List what is working. List what is not.

Circle three words that you want to define your leadership in the year ahead.
Post those words where you will see them every day. Then choose one action that brings those words to life this week.

The human heart of leadership has always been there. Reflection brings it back into focus. And from that focus, renewal grows and power returns to the place it belongs, within you.

Connect With Brianna

www.sylverconsulting.com
www.leadingthroughfreefall.com
www.linkedin.com/in/briannasylver
www.instagram.com/sylverconsulting

YOU DON'T NEED MORE GOALS, YOU NEED MORE ALIGNMENT

By **Iva Perez**
Cl. Hyp and Visibility Coach for Women Leaders

What Does a Panamanian Know About Hockey? (Apparently… Just Enough to Be Dangerous)

What does a Panamanian raised in the tropics know about ice and hockey?
Apparently… just enough to be dangerous. (Neuroscience dangerous, that is.)

The first time I saw snow, I was in college.
Gloves. Boots. Scarf. The whole *"I'm-a-tropical-girl-living-my-frosty-dream"* starter pack.

My friends, jaded by blizzards, rolled their eyes at me making snow angels.
But they also remember how my joy made them pause and slow down. Wonder makes you present.
And maybe that's why, when I later watched my first hockey game, I noticed something they didn't:
Some players didn't just chase the puck.
They *knew where it was going.*

That's not just sports.
That's neuroscience.

It's goal achievement 101.

Busy Is the New Boring

Most of us were trained to chase the puck.
We wear *busy* like it's Armani.
We glamorize hustle and answer every ping, every email, every child's *"Mooom!"* like speed equals safety.
We call the dopamine hit of *"done"* ambition.
Achievement got confused with aliveness.

The irony? That cortisol-fueled chase actually slows down your ability to achieve your goals.
When your brain runs on adrenaline, your prefrontal cortex, the part that gives you clarity and intuition, goes offline.
You're reacting to the last crisis instead of anticipating what's next.
You can't skate forward if your brain's still staring at the last puck.

That's not Gretzky-style flow.
That's firefighting.

Women have been running the world on cortisol for decades, and we wonder why our intuition feels muffled and our joy keeps buffering.

Alignment is the antidote.

Calm Is the Real Power Move

Flow isn't magic; it's chemistry.
It's dopamine, norepinephrine, and oxytocin syncing your body into coherence: a state where your nervous system, intuition, and focus line up like a symphony.

This energetic coherence is the *Two-Second Advantage* that separates the frantic from the focused.

You glide through your day like Gretzky across the ice, calm while everyone else scrambles.
You open your laptop and instantly know which email matters.
At meetings, your presence lands before your words do.

The Robe Theory

Women with wealth own robes.
Not because of the fabric, but because of what it represents: time that's theirs.

The first time I heard about this, it took me back to my corporate travel days when I'd slip into a hotel robe after endless meetings and finally feel myself exhale.

We traded ease for efficiency.
We made adrenaline a personality trait.
We sip caffeine like courage and call it balance.

But the robe doesn't ask you to do less.
It invites you to be more.
More coherent. More clear. More present.

Alignment isn't about slowing down; it's about syncing up.
It's not the absence of motion; it's *grace in motion*.

Your 2026 Alignment Blueprint

So, this December, before you write another resolution, ask yourself:

Do I want more goals?
Or do I want a nervous system that knows how to enjoy them?

Because goals were never about the *thing*, they were about the *feeling*.
The weight loss goal? You want to feel vibrant.
The income goal? Secure.
The family goal? Connected.

When your actions match your emotions and your emotions match your intentions, that's alignment.
That's flow.

Before rushing into 2026 with another list of *"shoulds,"* pause.
Breathe.
Wrap yourself in your metaphorical robe.
Let your nervous system catch up to your dreams.
Because alignment isn't about doing less, it's about *feeling* more alive while you do it.

Fewer goals and more *grace per goal*.
The most unstoppable woman in 2026 isn't the one skating faster.
She's the one finally skating to where her peace will be.

"Achievement got confused with aliveness. Alignment is the antidote."
"Less goals and more grace per goal. That's how unstoppable women rise."

Connect With Iva

www.linkedin.com/in/ivaperez
www.instagram.com/ivajperez

THE MID-DAY RESET:
WHY A DAILY WALK IS MY MOST POWERFUL TOOL FOR UNSTOPPABLE GROWTH

By **Phoebe Ng**

Let's be honest about the modern workday. We're trapped in a 9-hour, minimally-broken block of time. We're expected to be "*on*" from the moment we log in, straight through a "*lunch hour*" that most of us spend at our desks, clearing just enough email to feel like we're not drowning. By 3 PM, our brains are fried, our focus is gone, and our creativity is non-existent.

I live in this high-pressure world. As a leader in a fast-paced tech startup, the pull of a toxic, "*always-on*" culture is relentless. For a long time, I fought this by trying to be tougher—more coffee, more focus, more grit. It was a fast track to burnout.

My solution wasn't a new productivity app or a complex management system. It was a simple, non-negotiable 30-minute walk scheduled in the middle of every single day. This walk has become my most critical business practice—a powerful, purposeful act of self-care that fuels all my success.

The Power of the "*Mental Palate Cleanser*"

The morning is a creative and cognitive sprint. It's a flood of new tasks, urgent requests, and back-to-back meetings. By 1 PM, my brain is cluttered. Trying to power through the afternoon after eating a sandwich at my desk is like trying to paint a new picture on a canvas that's already full of wet paint. You just get mud.

My 30-minute walk acts as a "*mental palate cleanser.*" The simple act of physically stepping away from my workspace—out of the office, into the fresh air, with no phone calls—is a hard reset. It's a moment of active reflection where my brain can subconsciously process the morning's challenges and file them away. When I return to my desk, I'm not just slightly less tired; I am fundamentally reset. The mental fatigue is gone, and I have a clean, clear canvas for the afternoon.

Self-Care as a Strategic Boundary

For too long, corporate culture has sold us self-care as a luxury—a spa day, a "*mental health day,*" or a weekend retreat that you *earn* only after you've already hit the wall. This is a dangerous lie.

My daily walk is not a luxury. It is a firm, strategic boundary against an "*always-on*" culture that will take everything you are willing to give. It's a non-negotiable meeting with myself, scheduled in my calendar just like any other critical appointment. It is a purposeful action that protects my most valuable professional assets: my clarity, my energy, and my long-term mental health. You cannot be "*always on*" and also be a creative, empathetic, and effective leader.

From Reflection to Renewal

This is where this simple practice transforms from preventative to generative. My walk isn't just about *not* burning out; it's about actively fueling my creativity and growth.

When I am moving, with no agenda but to observe the world around me, my best ideas emerge. The solution to a complex marketing problem I was stuck on for an hour will suddenly appear. A new, more empathetic way to deliver feedback to my team will crystallize. This practice of mindfulness and movement is the engine of my renewal. It restores my focus and ensures that as the end-of-year pressure mounts, I can lead with a calm, clear head.

Unstoppable growth isn't about working more hours; it's about protecting the quality of the hours you do work. It's about having the wisdom to step away, reset, and return stronger.

Connect With Phoebe

www.linkedin.com/in/phoebe-yamin-ng
www.phoebe-yamin-ng.carrd.co
www.excelas.ai

FENIX TV
YOUR PLATFORM, YOUR VOICE, YOUR POWER

STEP INTO THE SPOTLIGHT AS A HOST ON FENIX TV!

Are you ready to amplify your message, inspire others, and be part of a groundbreaking network dedicated to empowering women worldwide? FENIX TV is your platform to shine as a host, share your expertise, and connect with a global audience.

WHY HOST ON FENIX TV?

- Reach a worldwide audience passionate about empowerment
- Showcase your voice, brand, and expertise
- Join a community of inspiring leaders and changemakers
- Be part of a network that uplifts and celebrates women

Whether you dream of leading a talk show, sharing powerful stories, or educating and inspiring others—FENIX TV is where your voice matters!

SECURE YOUR SPOT TODAY!

THE SHE RISES STUDIOS

PODCAST

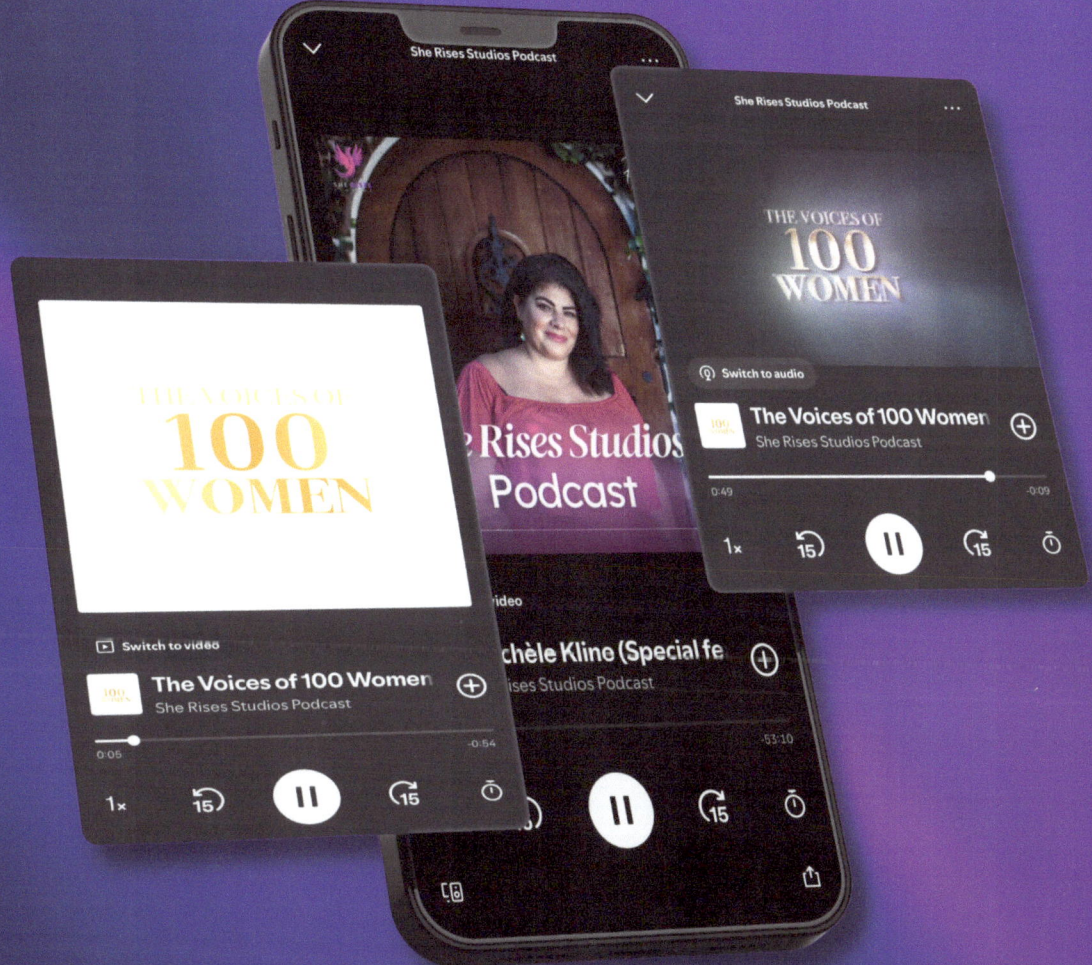

Each episode of the She Rises Studios Podcast delivers real stories, expert insights, and actionable strategies to help you step into your power and create the life you desire. This isn't just a podcast—it's your roadmap to confidence, success, and purpose.

Through powerful interviews with trailblazing entrepreneurs, thought leaders, and inspiring women, we dive deep into conversations that spark growth, fuel ambition, and ignite your potential. If you're ready to rise higher and live boldly, you're in the right place.

SUBSCRIBE NOW AND START YOUR JOURNEY TO EMPOWERMENT!

RESILIENCE THROUGH REINVENTION

By **Alice Anderson**

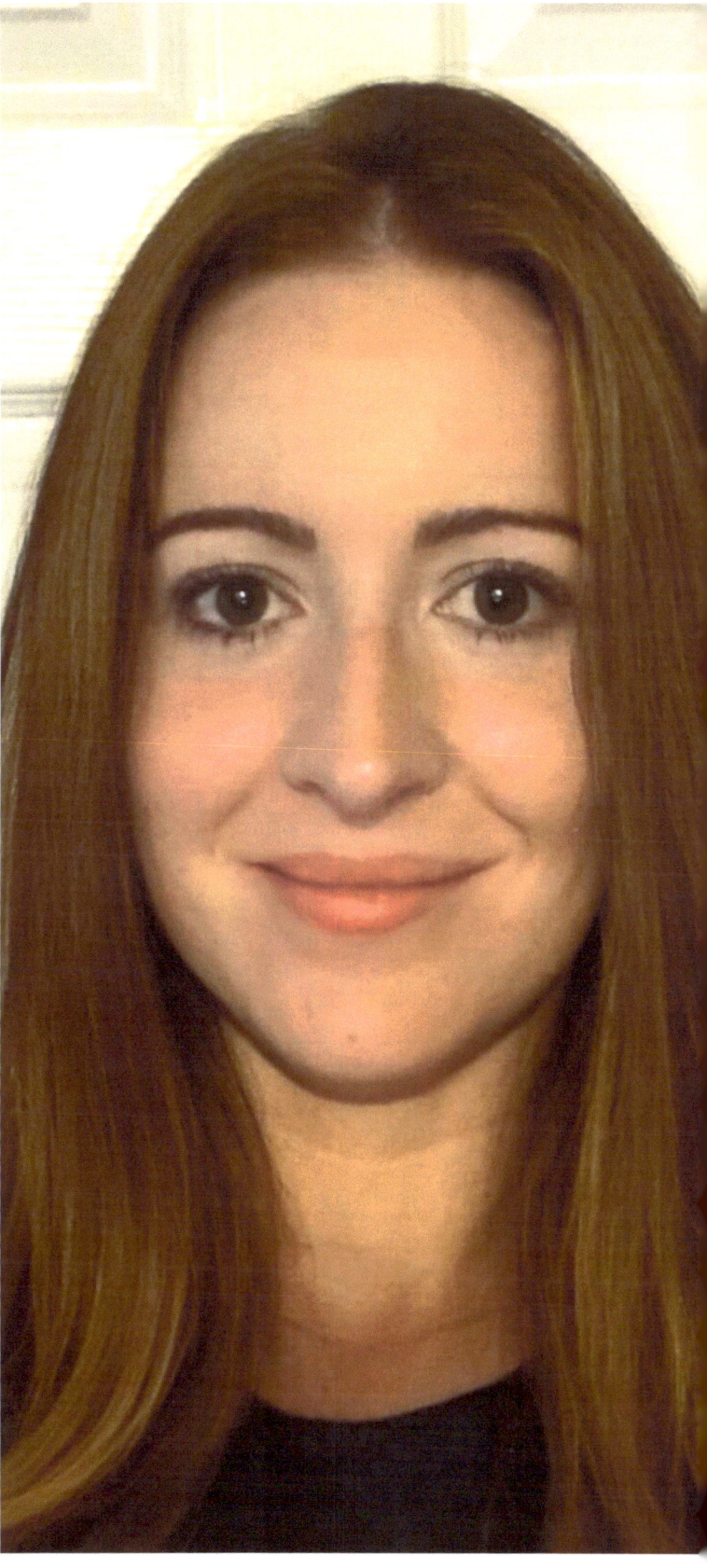

Change has a way of finding us whether we're ready or not. Sometimes it shows up as opportunity, other times as loss, but either way it asks the same question: who will you become next? Over the years I've learned that resilience isn't about never breaking. It's about how you rebuild after life shifts direction. Reflection is what helps you see the lesson, and renewal begins when you decide to start again.

I never imagined that reinvention would become such a constant part of my life. My first real job was as a dispatcher for a cable company. I loved the pace, the coordination, and the sense that I was helping things run smoothly behind the scenes. It was also where I met my husband. I thought that job would be my long-term path until the company closed its doors. Suddenly the routine I depended on disappeared. Instead of seeing that moment as a failure, I tried to treat it as an open door. I moved into insurance, where I quickly advanced from an entry-level position to more important roles.

A few years later, my husband and I got married, started a family, and made the decision that I would leave my full-time career to become a stay-at-home mom with our daughter and son. It was the right choice for us, but also a major identity shift. My sense of purpose had always been tied to my job. As my world expanded beyond my career, my purpose shifted toward nurturing my family and finding new ways to grow. Those years taught me patience, creativity, and flexibility, qualities that would later become the foundation of everything I built next.

Once both of my kids were in school, I felt a pull to create something of my own again. I didn't want to go back to the same kind of work, but I missed having goals outside of family life. I opened an Etsy shop with no big plan, just curiosity. That small experiment became the start of my third reinvention. I launched my own website and turned it into a full business centered on creativity, research, and content creation.

As I reflect on how far I've come, I see success in ways I never imagined years ago. My daughter is graduating high school fourth in her class, my son is thriving in middle school, and my website has reached millions of readers looking for the perfect team name. My husband and I have been married for 18 years, and the life we've built together is proof that resilience pays off. I still handle the stay-at-home duties and keep our household running, yet I've found a way to contribute financially and creatively. The greatest reward is the freedom to do meaningful work while still showing up for my family every day.

Connect With Alice

www.allteamnames.com

REFLECTION & RENEWAL:
THE POWER OF GRATITUDE FOR UNSTOPPABLE WOMEN

By **Mazhar Hussain**

As I reflect on my journey, I realize that gratitude has been the silent force guiding me through challenges, shaping my growth, and unlocking my potential. Life, as we all know, can be unpredictable. There are moments of joy, unexpected setbacks, and lessons that often feel too heavy to bear. Yet, it's in these very moments that I discovered the transformative power of self-awareness and reflection.

Embracing Self-Awareness

Self-awareness is more than just knowing your strengths and weaknesses—it's about understanding your emotions, your motivations, and the patterns that drive your decisions. I began journaling daily, asking myself simple yet powerful questions: What am I grateful for today? How can I transform this challenge into an opportunity? These reflections became a tool for clarity, helping me approach both personal and professional challenges with intention rather than reaction.

The Power of Gratitude

Gratitude is not just a feel-good exercise—it's a mindset that rewires your brain to see abundance instead of scarcity. When I consciously focused on what I had instead of what I lacked, doors I never imagined began to open. Simple acts, like thanking a colleague for their support or appreciating small wins in my business, created a ripple effect of positivity and motivation. Gratitude became my compass, guiding me through uncertainty with confidence and hope.

Turning Challenges into Growth

Every setback carries a lesson, and every obstacle presents an opportunity to grow. I remember a time when a major project I was passionate about faced unexpected hurdles. Initially, it felt like failure, but by reflecting on what went wrong and expressing gratitude for the lessons learned, I transformed the situation into a stepping stone for growth. Today, I view challenges as invitations to evolve, reminding myself that resilience is built one mindful choice at a time.

Mindful Renewal for a Purpose-Driven Life

Renewal is about consciously resetting your mindset, energy, and focus. I practice daily affirmations and morning prayers that center me before I start my day. These rituals are not mere routines—they are acts of self-care and empowerment. They remind me that no matter how busy life gets, prioritizing reflection and gratitude allows me to align my actions with my purpose. For unstoppable women preparing for a stronger 2026, mindful renewal is the secret ingredient to sustained success.

Actionable Steps to Cultivate Gratitude and Renewal

1. **Daily Journaling** – Spend 5–10 minutes reflecting on wins, challenges, and moments of gratitude.
2. **Mindful Breaks** – Pause during your day to appreciate small joys and acknowledge progress.
3. **Positive Affirmations** – Start each morning affirming your strengths, resilience, and vision.
4. **Reflective Conversations** – Share your journey with a mentor or friend to gain new insights.
5. **Celebrate Milestones** – Recognize both personal and professional achievements, no matter how small.

Closing Thoughts

Gratitude, reflection, and mindful renewal are not just practices—

they are a lifestyle that empowers women to transform obstacles into purpose and action. By embracing these principles, we cultivate resilience, clarity, and an unstoppable drive to create the life we envision. As I look ahead to 2026, I carry these lessons with me, committed to growing, inspiring, and supporting other women on their journeys.

Connect With Mazhar

www.infoblessings.com

By **Mazhar Hussain**

Introduction: Closing the Year With A Different Heart

As this year comes to a close, I find myself looking back not with regret, but with deep gratitude. Not because everything was perfect… but because I finally learned how powerful it is to pause, reflect, thank, and release. This year taught me that gratitude is not just an emotion it's a spiritual practice, a mindset shift, and a quiet inner decision to choose meaning over chaos. When I started looking at life through grateful eyes, everything began to feel lighter even the uncertainties.

Gratitude Is Not a Reaction It's A Daily Practice

Earlier in my journey, I used to be grateful only when something good happened. But real growth came when I started practicing gratitude intentionally even during silence, delays, setbacks, lessons, and unanswered prayers. Gratitude became my anchor.

It helped me slow down.
It helped me trust the timing.
It helped me appreciate the now not just chase the next.

Daily gratitude shifted me from *"why is this happening to me?"* into *"what is this teaching me?"* and that shift alone changed my energy, clarity, and confidence.

Reflection Helps You Release What You Don't Want To Carry Into The Next Year

Every year, we desire blessings, success, healing, new opportunities… but we forget that renewal requires release.

This year I learned to let go of:
- old expectations
- emotional baggage
- self-doubt
- past disappointments

Letting go is not weakness — it's self-respect. It creates space for new blessings to arrive. When I released what drained me, I became more aligned with who I truly want to be.

Gratitude Creates Inner Peace And Attraction Energy

I noticed something very real — when I practiced gratitude daily, I started attracting better experiences. Not magically, but mentally. When your mind is peaceful, you make better decisions. You communicate better. You respond wiser instead of reacting emotionally.

Gratitude is not only spiritual it is psychological, emotional, and practical. It reduces anxiety, improves focus, and builds resilience. It teaches you how to honor the present moment while preparing for a better future.

Stepping Into 2026 With A Renewed Spirit

2026 is not simply another year, it's a new chapter. And I want to enter it with alignment, not pressure. With gratitude, not comparison.

With peace, not panic. With intention, not fear.

So, to anyone reading this, I want to say:
You can't always control circumstances
but you can control your state of heart.

Start with one small practice daily:
Speak 3 things you're grateful for each morning.

That's how renewal begins, quietly, consistently, internally.

Gratitude is how I honor everything I lived through… and how I welcome everything that is coming next.

Connect With Mazhar

www.infoblessings.com

December 2025 AMAZON

COURAGEOUS Woman

Casting Cares Upon Jesus

COMPANION JOURNAL

CARMEN K. MAENDEL

HARNESSING GRATITUDE & REFLECTION FOR PERSONAL TRANSFORMATION

By **Mazhar Hussain**

When I reflect on this year, one powerful truth became clear: transformation doesn't happen only in big milestones, it often starts in those quiet moments when we pause and reflect. Gratitude became the anchor that shifted my mindset. Instead of chasing the next achievement, I began to honor the blessings already present in my life.

The Shift From Stress to Appreciation

Earlier, I would measure progress only by results and outcomes. But once I started recognizing small wins — a peaceful morning, a breakthrough idea, a lesson from a mistake — everything changed. Gratitude opened my eyes to the invisible growth that was happening within me. That was the moment I understood how mindset shapes identity.

Gratitude Creates Inner Confidence

Because when we acknowledge even tiny progress we no longer feel behind. We feel aligned.
Reflection Is the Bridge Between Who We Were & Who We Are Becoming
Reflection is not about judging the past, it is about understanding it.

Instead of asking:
"Why is this not happening yet?"

I now ask:
"What did this experience teach me?"

That question turned setbacks into wisdom.

This inner shift became the foundation of my personal transformation because reflection turns every season good or hard into meaningful data for the soul.

Why End-of-Year Reflection Matters for Women

As women, we carry emotional weight silently, expectations, dreams, responsibilities, disappointments. And most of the time, we forget to pause and appreciate the strength we already used to survive all of it.

Reflection reminds us:
We didn't just make it through another year we grew through it.

Renewal Is Not Reinventing Yourself It Is Returning to Your True Self

We didn't lose the best version of us, we simply paused her.
Reflection allows us to bring her back strong.

Closing the Year With Grace, Not Pressure

The end of the year is not about *"fixing everything fast."* It's about acknowledging the growth that happened quietly.

I am choosing to end this year with:
More gratitude than fear
More wisdom than worry
More renewal than rush

Because transformation is not a finish line it is a continuous unfolding.

My Final Reminder to You

You are not behind.
You are not late.
You are evolving beautifully.

Gratitude reminds you WHO you are.
Reflection reminds you WHERE you are going.
And that combination is the true power within.

Connect With Mazhar

www.infoblessings.com

SHE RISES STUDIOS

*U*NLEASH YOUR STORY

BECOME A PUBLISHED AUTHOR!

Have you ever dreamed of sharing your wisdom, experience, or passion with the world? **Now is your time!**

Publishing a book isn't just about writing—it's about **establishing your authority, inspiring others, and creating a lasting legac**y. Plus, with the **$138.5 billion book industry** booming, there's never been a better moment to step into the spotlight.

At **SRS Publishing**, we don't just publish books—we **elevate voices, empower authors, and create change-makers**. Our mission is to help women break barriers, amplify their stories, and thrive in the publishing world. Whether you're an entrepreneur, thought leader, or storyteller at heart, **we're here to guide you every step of the way.**

JOIN THE FASTEST-GROWING PUBLISHING HOUSE FOR WOMEN IN THE USA.

READY TO TURN YOUR DREAM INTO REALITY?

www.SheRisesStudios.com | contact@sherisesstudios.com

By **Dr. Tamea Ryan**

"Intentional" is everywhere. It's scribbled on journal covers, sprinkled into Instagram captions, and stitched into the language of self-development. Yet for a word that gets used so often, it's rarely explained in a way that feels honest or helpful.

What does it actually mean to live an intentional day? Not the Pinterest version. Not the hyper-optimized routine. The real version, especially for people navigating burnout, grief, and deep change.

Here's how I define it.

Intentional Doesn't Mean Perfect
Having an intentional day doesn't mean you followed a perfect schedule, meditated at 6 a.m., and checked everything off your to-do list. It means you made choices aligned with who you are becoming, rather than staying stuck in who you used to be. It's not about performing presence. It's about practicing it.

Decisions From Autopilot
So many people are living on autopilot. They're making decisions based on outdated patterns, old expectations, and inherited stories. Not because they're lazy. Because they're trying to survive. The problem is that autopilot decisions tend to reinforce who you've been and not who you're becoming. You wake up one day with a calendar full of responsibilities that feel like someone else's life. That's why intentionality matters.

Alignment Over Achievement
At its core, intentionality is about alignment. It asks you to pause long enough to ask: *"Is this decision aligned with the person I'm becoming?"* Sometimes the answer leads to big changes. Sometimes it leads to small shifts, such as skipping an event, saying no to a plan, turning off your phone. What matters is that your actions start to reflect your values, not your fears.

What It Looks Like in Real Life
An intentional day might look like:
- Letting yourself sleep in because your body needs rest.
- Turning down a project that pays well but drains your spirit.
- Saying yes to something that scares you, not because it's easy but because it's time.
- Letting go of pressure to do things perfectly and doing them honestly instead.

Permission to Reclaim Your Day
"Intentionality isn't something you earn once you have your life."

It's something you practice in the middle of the mess. It's choosing to listen to yourself more closely than you listen to pressure. It's choosing to design your day, even one small part of it, in a way that reflects the life you're building, not just the life you've inherited. Some days that looks like clarity. Other days it looks like grace. Most days, it looks like trying again.

You Don't Have to Earn It
You don't have to earn rest. You don't have to prove your worth through productivity. You don't have to make every hour count to count as a person. Living an intentional day starts with believing that your story deserves care now not just when it's finished or successful or fully healed.

The Bottom Line
Intentional days are not curated. They are created imperfectly, quietly, and without applause. They begin when you decide to stop moving from obligation and start moving from alignment.

So if today you:
- Pause instead of pushing,
- Reflect instead of reacting,
- Choose honesty over habit…

Then that is an intentional day, and it is enough.

Connect With Dr. Tamea
www.thelivedexp.com
www.instagram.com/thelivedexp
www.facebook.com/TheLivedExperiences

RESILIENCE THROUGH REINVENTION:
RISING FROM THE ASHES OF CHANGE

By **Brenda *"Bre"* Bardaels, PsyD (c)**

Every January, I start with intention. As a doctoral researcher, Army National Guard officer, and woman determined to grow with purpose, I began 2025 with one clear goal: finish and defend my dissertation proposal. I had spent months studying leadership and psychological safety to understand how people rebuild trust after adversity. What I didn't know was that my year would become a living experiment in resilience itself.

In early January, the Palisades fires broke out across California, and my plans were instantly transformed. Overnight, I traded academic writing for field gear, answering the call to serve as part of the California Army National Guard's response team. For weeks, our mission was to provide relief, structure, and safety amid chaos. Flames consumed not only homes but dreams, plans, and a sense of normalcy. Families were displaced; communities were shattered.

Amid the ashes, I learned what it truly means to pivot with purpose.

Reinvention Is Not Failure. It's Evolution

In my book Not Your Average Leader, I wrote that leadership begins where comfort ends. Reinvention, like leadership, demands surrender, letting go of what we thought life should look like so we can discover what it can become.

During the fires, I learned that resilience isn't about *"bouncing back."* It's about building forward. I carved out moments in my tent to revise my dissertation proposal by flashlight. Some nights, I wrote while exhaustion blurred the words. Other nights, I reminded myself that persistence is its own form of healing. When I finally got to come home and defended my proposal successfully, it was an academic milestone and a declaration of survival.

The truth is reinvention often begins when our old plans no longer fit the person we are becoming. For many of us women balancing careers, families, studies, or service, this past year demanded a courage we didn't know we had. Some lost homes or jobs; others faced burnout or transitions that forced them to redefine success. I see these women not as broken but as reborn, reshaped by fire, refined by purpose.

Reflection as a Tool for Renewal

Resilience requires reflection. During quiet moments after deactivation, I began journaling, something I encourage every woman to do. Reflection turns experience into wisdom. It helps us see patterns, name our growth, and forgive ourselves for what didn't go as planned.

Ask yourself: What did this season teach me? What must I release to move forward?

The answers may surprise you. Sometimes the greatest renewal comes not from adding more to your life, but from releasing what no longer serves your peace.

The Power Within

When the fires died down, many of us began rebuilding, not just homes, but identities. I returned to my research with deeper empathy and purpose. My dissertation, which explores how destructive leadership impacts psychological safety, now feels more urgent than ever. Because resilience isn't built in isolation;

it grows in the spaces where leaders nurture trust, compassion, and inclusion.

For every woman closing out 2025 feeling weary, uncertain, or stretched thin, remember this: renewal is not a luxury, it's a necessity. Reinvention is not the end of your story; it's the rewriting of its draft.

Sometimes life's fires don't destroy us, they illuminate the path to who we were meant to become.

Connect With Bre

www.notyouraverageleaderbook.com
Instagram: @Bre_At_Losal

INTERVIEW WITH ALISON MCBAIN, FOUNDER OF THE AUTHORS VS AI PROJECT

Interview conducted by **Danielle Urban** of **AR Critique**
https://elarcritique.wordpress.com/about/

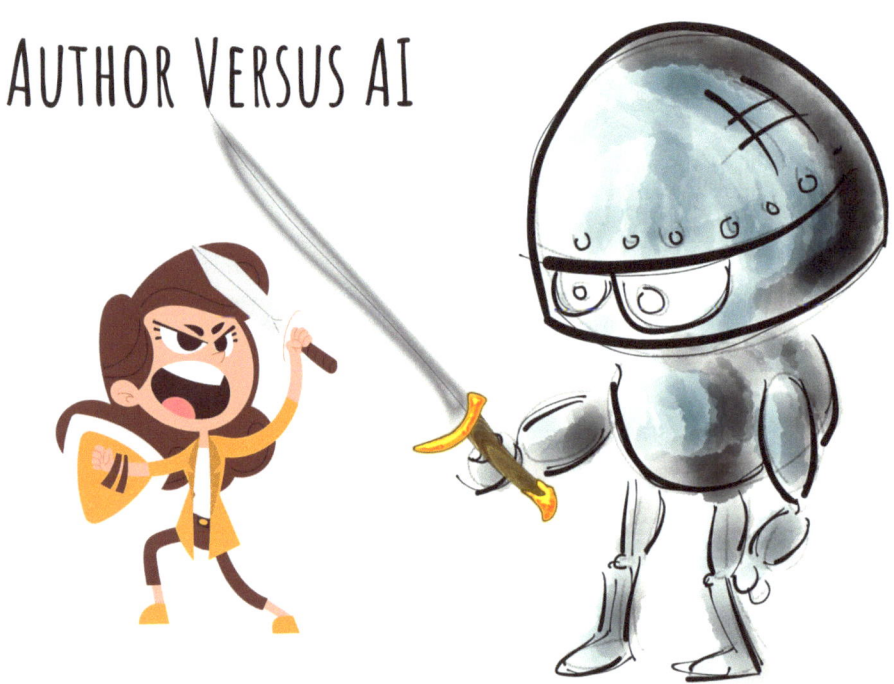

Q: What is the big deal of introducing AI to the book industry?

Like any new technology, there are benefits and drawbacks to some of the ways AI has developed. Benefit: programs such as Grammarly or spellcheck, which can help authors proofread their work. Drawbacks: (1) Advanced AI programs have been trained on authors' writings without the authors' permission at all, which has resulted in several lawsuits (***https://www.reuters.com/legal/pulitzer-winning-authors-join-openai-microsoft-copyright-lawsuit-2023-12-20/***). (2) AI writing programs produce substandard work, including writing that has strange emotional reactions and stilted dialogue. (3) There's the question of who is profiting from this. It's certainly not the writers, either the ones whose work is being used without their permission or the ones who are using AI to create substandard books. So, who are the ones receiving financial gain from this? It's not the little guy. And if it's just big companies increasing their profit margin… no, thank you.

Q: Should authors be worried about the use of AI?

Yes and no. Right now—no. AI won't replace human writers for the most part, especially in the fiction genre. It can be used to assist writers; for example, a number of writers might use it to help them produce book summaries for their work, and companies are using it to write nonfiction copy. But when it comes to the creative act of producing realistic and enthralling fiction, it's not currently a threat.

However, that doesn't mean it won't be one in the future. The thing with new technology is that it always has a lot of bugs and drawbacks when it first appears. But then it gets better... and better. Engineers and programmers find ways around the problems.

Look at cell phones today and compare them to the first commercial computers in the 1950s-1970s. There's no comparison—cell phones run circles around those computers from just a few decades ago. What was science fiction back then (for example, tricorders, communicators, and universal translators from Star Trek) has become a reality to us now.

So, I think that AI will get better. It is a threat to creative pursuits everywhere, since it takes what authors and other creatives love to do and cuts out the human element and makes it solely about profit.

Q: Will human creativity win over the talent of the AI programs?

Right now, yes. AI programs create strange emotional reactions in characters they write, and use bland or strange language that might be technically accurate but doesn't ring true for people reading it. It's the whole idea of the *"uncanny valley,"* where people can see a robot that looks human but know that it's not human. There's something *"off"* about it. Same with AI's writing—sure, it's words. But they're not the right words and they usually end up falling flat.

Q: Why do you believe that authors would be favorable in using AI to write their books versus using their own real strengths? Would publishers know the difference?

As a publisher myself of a small literary magazine, I'll answer yes—we can completely tell the difference between human writing and AI. Some authors, however, will look for shortcuts in writing their books, since writing can be a long and hard endeavor. If you've been writing your book for half a year, a year, ten years... it might be tempting to think: *"Oh, I can just plug this into a program and ask it to finish the book for me instantaneously."*

However, that's the problem—it's not your work then. Great literature is great because someone put the work into it. It's just like a meal from a 5-star restaurant versus the mass-produced frozen food from the grocery store. Both might be food, but there's a significant difference between the two.

Q: Tell us, readers, about your book, Author vs AI.

My project Author Versus AI is one author (me) showing that authors can write almost as fast as AI, but much, much better. Over the course of a year—from Global Book Day (April 23) in 2024 to Global Book Day in 2025, I'm writing a book a week. At the end of this project, I hope to have 52 books in a wide range of genres. I'm tackling everything from mystery to romance, science fiction to comedy, and there's even a nonfiction book and some short story collections thrown in there.

And so far, so good. I've been completing the books and moving onto the next genre. I'm having a lot of fun tackling new stories every week, but I will probably be VERY tired by the end of this project and might not want to look at words for a while, ha.

Q: As an editor is the AI good or bad for the publishing industry?

If AI is used as a tool to help writers and editors, it can absolutely be good. It can help cut down on the tedium of producing marketing material for authors, which is something authors often do instead of spending their valuable time writing new books. It can help with spelling and grammar and make an editor's job easier when they receive an author's manuscript if the author has first run their work through an editing software program.

However, if it's used to replace writers and artists and editors and the myriad of other creative professionals whose experience goes into producing top quality books, then I feel the industry will suffer. Right now, it can't replace what people do. It just can't—I've read manuscripts that have been checked over by editing software, and they have plenty of awkward sentences and uneven pacing, as well as some typos (for example, a recent manuscript I edited had errors such as confusing the name *"Cain"*—from the Bible—and replacing it with *"Cane"*). That's something only a human editor can catch. I've also read short stories produced by AI programs and they're badly written. Neither one holds a candle to a human writer or human editor.

AI is a new and trendy fad, and one that a lot of publishers, especially small press publishers, are turning against. But I think one major thing will determine what impact AI has on the industry, and that's profitability. The publishing model has been changing for a while with the advent of cheap self-publishing and print-on-demand. However, self-published authors have still struggled to make as significant an impact on readers as traditionally published authors. And that's because there's a lack of gatekeepers to make sure the quality is standardized across self-published work. There can be fabulous self-published books that are well-written and edited, and there can be simply abysmal ones. But it's sometimes hard to tell which is which before you start reading the book.

I think the advent of AI will make this trend accelerate. People will be pumping out AI-generated books with the idea that they can make a fast profit—the whole *"something for nothing"* mentality. I've seen it myself at my literary magazine, where we get spammed by dozens of submissions that are obviously AI-generated, even though our guidelines specifically say no AI.

So, what this means for the industry is that it will make things harder for the little guy. It will be harder for small presses to regulate and survive if they have to deal with an overwhelming quantity of submissions by a few bad apples. It reminds me of the early days of email before spam was really a thing. Now, there are all kinds of spam emails, including by fraudsters trying the steal your information. I think AI writing and scams will become more and more advanced in the same way, and the gatekeepers—such as those trying to prevent plagiarism—will become overwhelmed and unable to keep up.

Q: Where do you see the future of writers using their own words versus those that use AI to write for them?

I think there will always be demand for writers who don't use AI. Authors write for the love of it and to share in the human experience, so I think that our words will resonate in ways that AI writing can't right now... or perhaps won't ever be able to, at least in the near future.

I think AI will become useful in nonfiction writing, such as writing website copy, instruction manuals, and the like. Because it tends to be emotionless and factual, it will work better in those fields rather than in fiction, which needs subtlety and a range of emotional reactions from the characters.

Q: What other projects are you currently working on at the moment?

Writing 52 books in a year should be enough for me, but I'm actually working on a few other things at the same time.

One, I'm the publisher for the magazine ScribesMICRO (*https://www.fairfieldscribes.com/*), which publishes very short fiction, poetry, and creative nonfiction once a month. We're about to start taking submissions for our annual contest, The Scribes Prize (*https://www.fairfieldscribes.com/the-scribes-prize.html*), which offers cash prizes to the top 18 writers. Top prize is $250.

Two, my press Fairfield Scribes is publishing the fabulous horror novel Designs of Death in October by debut author Micah C. Brown. Stephen King said of Brown's writing that he has *"a real storyteller's knack."*

Three, I regularly write articles about writing, as well as short stories and poems on the writing platform Medium (*https://medium.com/@amcbain*) and publish essays, fiction, and poetry on Vocal (*https://vocal.media/authors/alison-mc-bain*).

Q: Where can readers find you and your work online?

The two main places where you can reach me are my website: *https://www.alisonmcbain.com/* and my Author Versus AI website: *http://www.authorversusai.com/*. All my social media links are on those two websites, so follow me, tweet at me, or Tok to me anytime you want.

Connect With Alison

www.alisonmcbain.com
www.facebook.com/alison.mcbain.9
www.twitter.com/AlisonMcBain
www.instagram.com/alisonamcbain
www.linkedin.com/in/alison-mcbain-0a026a266
www.youtube.com/channel/UCm9PMu4p4urp_un0oy1vroQ

HARO connects journalists with sources for stories.

Journalists, submit a query to connect with sources.

SUBSCRIBE FOR FREE DAILY MEDIA QUERIES.

WWW.HELPAREPORTER.COM

By **Liisa Kovala**

Ever wondered why Finland has been named the happiest country in the world for eight consecutive years based on the World Happiness Report? I could argue it's the amount of coffee they drink—about four cups per person per day or twenty-six pounds per person per year—or perhaps it's the proximity to nature, the social support and services, or the work life balance. All of this may be true, but I think their happiness stems from something even more fundamental and something we can all benefit from in our daily lives: sisu.

Sisu is a cultural concept that gained world recognition during the Finnish-Russian Winter War of 1939-1940 when this small country defended itself from its neighbour with great success. The Winter War continues to be the prime example of how Finnish soldiers with their lack of military equipment and few soldiers were able to stave off the advances of the Soviet Union. The term doesn't have a specific English translation, but has variously been described as courage, determination, grit, and bravery in the face of adversity. But it goes beyond resilience. When it looks like the outcome is impossible, and one is likely to fail, Finns keep going. That's sisu.

The word sisu is derived from the original word sisus, literally meaning guts. It first appeared in writing in the sixteenth century with negative connotations but has survived for centuries. Over time, the term became more positively associated with fortitude and an unwillingness to give up. Today, sisu is the foundation of the Finnish character.

As a Finnish Canadian, I grew up with the concept, intrinsically understanding what it meant. Sisu applied to everyday life, from pushing oneself to finish a race, picking oneself up after failing a test, or completing that math homework that just seemed so impossible. Now, as an adult, I regularly draw on my sisu when I'm faced with personal problems, professional situations, or challenges in the world that I can't control. There is an element of pulling oneself up by one's bootstraps, but there is something else, too. It's a quiet, underlying strength. A deep knowledge and understanding that we have it within ourselves to continue, to move forward, to succeed.

While Finns lay claim to the concept of sisu, I believe everyone has it within themselves. We just need to access our sisu to benefit from its power. There are many ways one can find this quiet fortitude and it's simpler than you think. Find your sisu by doing what the Finns do.

- **Take a walk in nature.** There is something magical about breathing fresh air, moving one's body, and noticing the sounds and scents around you. Walking clears your mind, sparks your creativity, and elicits problem-solving.
- **Take a sauna.** Did you know Finland has over 3 million saunas and there is one sauna for roughly every 1.5 people? The sauna is a place to clear one's mind as well as body, reflect, think deeply, and gain inner strength. Add a plunge into cold water or an ice bath to rejuvenate oneself.
- **Relax.** In addition to walking and taking a sauna, find other ways to relax. In our hustle culture, it's difficult to find moments to truly relax without thinking about our to-do list or scrolling on our phones. Relaxing means shutting off the external world and entering the internal world. Sisu is there within you. Breathe. You will find it.
- **Challenge yourself.** Do hard things. It's easy to find the comfortable path, but it won't lead you to where you want to go.
- **Lean on others.** You don't have to do things alone. Find support in friends, family, and colleagues. Share the load and find your strength in working together.
- **Don't give up.** That's easier said than done. When faced with challenges, it's easy to tell ourselves we can't do it. The truth is, we can. Shut down the inner critic who is trying to protect us from the unknown and listen to that inner champion who knows anything is possible. That's sisu talking.

Success, whatever that looks like to individuals, relies on a variety of factors, including hard work, determination, and often a bit of luck. But don't forget about what's been in you the whole time. Sisu will see you through the difficult times, will drive you forward, will forge a path when it feels impossible.

Close your eyes. Breathe. Feel your sisu deep inside you. It's always been there. Once you've found it, you'll remember it was always there. Your sisu will lead you to that calm feeling of internal strength that will help find success, and I think, happiness, too.

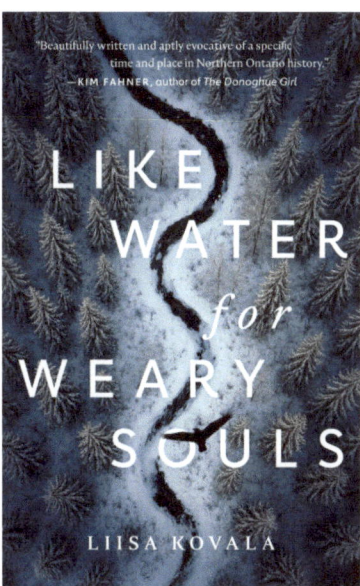

Connect With Liisa

www.liisakovalabookcoach.com
www.instagram.com/liisakovala
www.facebook.com/liisakovalawriter
www.youtube.com/channel/UCur2N9JMaRpLpJS8vORE8Cw

she wins
WOMEN'S NETWORK

Elevate your business with the power of community.

Get access to the tools, connections, and support you need to grow—with a circle of women who truly get it.

WHAT'S INCLUDED

- Strategic networking & mentorship
- Expert-led masterclasses & exclusive resources
- Member spotlights, VIP perks & more

Join for just
$87/MONTH
no contracts, cancel anytime.

www.shewinswomensnetwork.com

JOIN THE SHE RISES STUDIOS COMMUNITY

SCAN TO JOIN

Daily motivation, expert insights, and sisterhood support come together in one empowering space. Connect, empower, and thrive—whether you're an entrepreneur, professional, or simply seeking inspiration, this is your place to grow!

You don't have to do it alone—let's rise together!

BUILDING PEACE FROM WITHIN:
A CALL TO RECONCILIATION IN A DIVIDED WORLD

By **CC Robinson**

In an age defined by division, the question of how to avoid war and conflict, whether between nations, communities, or people, has never been more urgent. The truth is, peace is not negotiated only in political chambers or international summits; it is built in the quiet, deliberate choices we make every day. It begins with the courage to see one another fully, especially when it feels impossible.

True reconciliation requires more than tolerance; it demands transformation. It asks us to examine the wars within; the resentment, fear, and judgment that separate us from one another. If we do not heal those inner battles, they inevitably spill outward. Racial reconciliation, like all forms of peacemaking, is not a single moment of agreement but a lifelong discipline of humility and hope.

When we talk about avoiding war, we are really talking about choosing connection over control. Every conflict, large or small, begins with the belief that my story matters more than yours — that my pain deserves to be heard first. But healing begins when we decide that everyone's story matters equally. It begins when we stop speaking only to be right and start listening to understand.

I learned this truth most vividly in Sierra Leone, where I traveled a dozen times as a medical doctor between 2004 and 2012. The nation was still emerging from nearly thirty years of brutal civil war, and I expected to find only gaping wounds. Instead, I witnessed extraordinary forgiveness and grace. I remember speaking with a UN peacekeeper who told me, *"The people of Sierra Leone have laid down not only the guns in their hands, but the guns in their hearts."*

That statement shaped everything I saw afterward. I watched men who had killed each other's families — men who had committed atrocities in each other's villages — forgive one another. They were working side by side to rebuild homes, clinics, and schools. These were not abstract gestures of peace; they were acts of radical humanity. They taught me that reconciliation is not forgetting what was done, but choosing to live forward despite it. They showed me that even the deepest wounds can become the soil for renewal.

Avoiding war does not mean avoiding conflict. In fact, peacebuilders know that healthy tension is part of the process. It's in those uncomfortable conversations that the possibility of understanding begins to emerge. Courage is not the absence of fear; it's choosing to stay engaged in relationship and choosing to act in compassion and love even when fear arises.

For women, especially those of us who lead in our communities, we have a vital role to play in this work. We are often the first to notice the fractures in our families, workplaces, and communities. We can also be the first to imagine how they might be healed. The world needs that vision. It needs women who refuse to let cynicism harden their hearts, who see possibility where others see brokenness.

The work of reconciliation is not glamorous. It rarely earns applause. But it changes everything. Each act of empathy is a seed of peace. Each time we choose to forgive, just like those men did in Sierra Leone, we disarm the invisible weapons that threaten our shared humanity.

Avoiding war starts with asking better questions: How can I show up differently?

Where can I build bridges instead of walls? Who have I refused to see clearly? The answers are rarely simple, but they can and will lead to change.

The path toward peace is slow, imperfect, and deeply human. Yet every step matters. Every conversation matters. Every brave act of love and truth-telling moves us closer to the world we all long for — one where justice and mercy walk hand in hand.

If we are to become unstoppable women in a world that often feels unsteady, we must anchor ourselves in compassion and forgiveness. We must commit to being both strong and soft, bold and kind. Because the future of peace depends not just on policies or institutions. No, the future of our world depends on people like us, choosing every day to love louder than hate.

Connect With CC

www.ccrobinsonauthor.com
www.instagram.com/ccrobinsonauthor
www.facebook.com/ccrobinsonauthor
www.tiktok.com/@ccrobinsonauthor
www.threads.net/ccrobinsonauthor

RISING ABOVE THE "OUTDATED VERSION" OF MYSELF

By **Yuliana Francie**

In every season of life, we arrive at a fork-in-the-road moment—a choice between fear or love. But these options rarely present themselves clearly. Often, adversity doesn't appear as disaster, loss, or catastrophe. Instead, it arrives disguised as *success.* It comes dressed as the life you thought you wanted, the relationship that *"checks all the boxes,"* or the career you built by being everything to everyone.

On my long flight home from Las Vegas after presenting at the She Wins Summit, a movie caught my attention: Materialists.

And within it, the story of Lucy Mason—a matchmaker in the glittering swirl of New York City—became a mirror.

Lucy's adversity didn't show up through failure; it arrived through *illusion.*

A failed actress turned successful matchmaker, Lucy spent years crafting other people's happily-ever-afters while quietly doubting she'd ever receive her own. She hid her fear of being alone behind polished pitches, curated matches, and the fantasy of marrying someone wealthy. To the world, she looked confident, accomplished, and composed. But inside, she was exhausted from carrying an identity built on expectations rather than truth.

Her defining moment wasn't losing a job, a home, or a relationship.
Her defining moment was losing *herself.*

Like many women, it happened gradually—one compromise, one silenced intuition, one *"be reasonable"* at a time. She ignored clients' unrealistic standards. She ignored the guilt when one of her matches went wrong. And she ignored her own heart when she stepped into a relationship that was perfect on paper but empty in reality.

When Harry, a wealthy financier, pursued her, she convinced herself that ticking boxes was the same as building a real connection. He was generous, successful, and socially polished—the kind of man she believed she was supposed to want. But adversity has a way of revealing the places where we've abandoned ourselves.

For Lucy, her truth cracked open when she found an engagement ring hidden in Harry's luggage—right beside the revelation that he had spent $200,000 surgically altering his height to feel *"good enough."*

In that moment, she saw the mirror with painful clarity: both of them were trying to be chosen for who they weren't. That clarity became her turning point.

Rising above an outdated version of yourself requires choosing truth over approval, alignment over expectation, love over status. It meant telling a good man the hardest truth: *We are not in love. We are in love with an idea—an idea suffocating us both.*

Walking away wasn't dramatic or explosive. It was quiet, reverent, and profoundly brave—like all genuine transformations.

But her deepest rise came later, when she faced Sophie, the client harmed by one of her matches. Even after being told to stay away for legal reasons, Lucy chose integrity over convenience. She apologized—not as a businesswoman protecting her brand, but as a woman waking up to the cost of self-abandonment. Sophie lashed out, but even that was part of rising: standing in truth without demanding instant forgiveness.

Her greatest liberation came when she reconnected with John—the man she once left because he didn't meet her checklist. Confronting him meant confronting herself. It meant acknowledging that she once valued financial security more than emotional truth. And it meant realizing that the love she dismissed was the love that saw her most clearly.

She rose above adversity the moment she chose authenticity over aspiration, emotional wealth over financial optics, and connection over performance.

Rising above adversity isn't always about conquering external battles—it's about shedding the identity that no longer fits.

Lucy's story is a reminder to every woman:
You become unstoppable the moment you stop contorting yourself for a life that doesn't honour who you truly are.

It is not success that makes you unstoppable.
It is self-honesty.
It is self-trust.
It is the courage to choose the life that feels like home, not the one that looks good on paper.

Sovereignty isn't a role you claim—it is the embodiment of your truth.
And when you step fully into who you really are, life opens doors that were always meant for you.

For me, one of those doors was standing on the She Wins Summit stage, reminding women what it feels like to reconnect with their true selves, to remember their power, and to build their business and lifestyle from a place of deep inner alignment.

That is the moment I rose above *my* outdated version.
And like Lucy, I chose the woman I was becoming.

If this resonates with you… your evolution has already begun.

My book *Unbecoming You* is your next step, a 21-day journey to shed the identities that no longer serve you and step into the woman you were always meant to be.

Check out *Unbecoming You* and start your transformation today.

Connect With Yuliana

www.yulianafrancie.com/unbecoming
www.linkedin.com/in/yulianafrancie
www.facebook.com/yuliana.francie11

SHOP NOW | FUNCHO.CO

SHIFTING FEAR INTO EXCITEMENT:
YOUR SECRET MINDSET SHIFT FOR SUCCESS

By **Hannah Darby**

Have you ever noticed how fear and excitement feel strangely similar in your body?

Your heart races, your palms get sweaty, you feel a little shaky, a little wired, like something big is about to happen.

That's not an accident, it's biology.

When we're nervous, our body activates the same stress response system (the sympathetic nervous system) that's involved in excitement.

Heart rate increases, breathing changes, and adrenaline rises, whether you're about to speak on stage or step onto a rollercoaster.

The difference isn't in your body, it's in the story your mind tells about what those sensations mean. That's where your most powerful mindset shift for success lives:
Instead of telling yourself *"I'm scared"*… **you start telling yourself** *"I'm excited."*

The science behind *"I'm excited"*

Psychological research has shown that when people reframe their anxiety as excitement, literally by saying "I'm excited" out loud, they perform better on stressful tasks like public speaking, a maths tests, or singing in front of others. The arousal in the body is the same, it's the label that changes the outcome. In other words, your body is gearing up to help you rise to the moment, not run from it.

Fear says: *This is dangerous. I'm not safe.*
Excitement says: *This matters. I'm ready to grow.*

That tiny shift in wording can move you from paralysis into possibility.

Why fear shows up when you're on the brink of something good

Fear isn't proof you're on the wrong path; more often, it's proof you're growing.

We feel fear when we're:
- Visible in new ways (sharing a story, launching a business, raising our prices)
- Stepping out of the familiar (career change, new relationship, relocating)
- Claiming more for ourselves (success, joy, love, money, freedom)

Your nervous system reads *"new"* as *"uncertain"*, and uncertain can feel unsafe, making your alarm bells ring. But often, those bells are really saying:
"You're standing at the edge of expansion."

When you start to relate to those sensations as excitement, as your body *preparing* you, everything softens. You don't have to get rid of the feeling; you just have to reinterpret it.

A simple 3-step shift: from fear to excitement

You can try this before a big conversation, a presentation, a first session with a client, or any moment that feels high-stakes.

1. Notice the signals.
Pause and name what you feel physically:
- *"My heart is racing."*
- *"My chest feels tight."*
- *"My stomach is fluttering."*

Instead of *"I feel awful,"* get curious: *What's my body actually doing?*

2. Change the story.
Gently choose a new label:
- *"My heart is racing because I care."*
- *"This rush is energy, I'm excited."*
- *"My body is giving me fuel for this moment."*

You can even say out loud: **"I'm excited about this."** It might feel clunky at first, but that's okay. You're rewiring a habit.

3. Channel the energy.
Fear tends to freeze us. Excitement wants to move.
Use that surge on purpose:
- Take a few deeper, slower breaths to anchor your nervous system.

© VANDA SZABO PHOTOGRAPHY

- Roll your shoulders, shake out your hands, stand up taller.
- Ask yourself: *If I really believed this was excitement, what's one bold action I'd take next?*

Then do that one thing. Send the email, hit *"post"*, say *"yes."*

You don't have to wait until you're *"not scared"*

One of the biggest myths about success is that confident people don't feel fear. However, they do, they just don't wait for fear to disappear before they act.

They learn to:
- Walk alongside it
- Translate it into excitement
- Use it as a sign they're moving toward something meaningful

Next time your stomach flips before a big step, try whispering to yourself:
"This is my body cheering me on."

Because often, the difference between *"I can't do this"* and *"I'm ready for this"* isn't a different life or a different past.

It's the same heartbeat, the same shaky hands…and a new story:
I'm not scared, I'm excited, and I'm doing it anyway.

Connect With Hannah

www.healingwithhannah.co.uk
www.facebook.com/healingwithhannahdarby
www.instagram.com/healingwithhannahd
www.linkedin.com/in/hannahdarbyhealingwithhannah
www.youtube.com/@HealingwithHannah-hwh

100 WOMEN OF IMPACT™

THE DOCUSERIES THAT AMPLIFIES WOMEN'S VOICES

We just wrapped our first taping of 100 Women of Impact™ in San Diego, and the momentum has only just begun. This powerful docuseries is shining a spotlight on extraordinary women who are shaping the future through leadership, resilience, and influence.

Be part of the movement by sharing your story in an exclusive filmed interview for the docuseries. Gain visibility through red carpet experiences, media coverage, and distribution across She Rises Studios platforms, while connecting with a global network of women making an unstoppable impact.

NEXT FILMING OPPORTUNITIES

SHE WINS GLOBAL SUMMIT | LAS VEGAS | NOVEMBER 6–7, 2025
EMPOWERHER CONTENT DAY | LAS VEGAS | FEBRUARY 2026

SIGN UP TODAY

VISIT WWW.SHERISESSTUDIOS.COM/INTRODUCING-100-WOMEN-OF-IMPACT TO CLAIM YOUR SPOT.

ENROLL FREE TODAY TO SCALE YOUR BUSINESS

She Rises Studios and Goldman Sachs 10,000 Women join forces to provide education, resources, and a supportive global community for women-led SMEs, empowering them to grow, innovate, and thrive in today's competitive landscape.

MAKE IT A NEW YEAR!

By **Tiffany Tyler-Garner, PhD**

It is 2026! As we begin this new year, make sure it is really a new year! Commit to doing new things this year. Whether it is applying new strategies or approaches, or beginning a new practice or opportunity, this is a great time to make your year new by doing something new. Don't be content with being on the sidelines of your life and don't accept the complacency characterized by:

- Just getting by.
- Barely making ends meet.
- Going along to get along.
- Letting others set the bar for your joy, peace, or health.

You deserve a year filled with abundance. Moreover, you deserve a life that exemplifies the potential, gifts, and talents that you bring to every table and this world. If you are not consistently experiencing a quality of life indicative of your hopes, dreams, and vision, let this new year be a new opportunity to do it.

As a first step, take stock of all you've been doing and ask yourself:

- Am I beginning this year where I hoped in my:
  - Physical health?
  - Financial health?
  - Mental health?
  - Emotional health?
  - Social health?
  - Occupational health?
  - Spiritual health?
- Am I realizing the vision I have for my life, including the vision I have for my:
  - Relationships?
  - Career?
  - Finances?
  - Health
  - Home?
- Are my choices, thinking, beliefs, and mindset serving me well?
- Am I building the legacy I envision?
- Am I consistently communicating, collaborating, coordinating, and decision-making effectively?
- Am I leading myself and others effectively?
- If I died today, would my obituary reflect the life, leadership, and legacy I hope to contribute to the world?
- If I died today, am I more likely to die with regret, revelation, reservations, or reward?

- If I spent this year doing what I did last year, would I be further ahead or further behind?
- If my children or others followed my example, would they be successful?

If your answers to any of these questions are inconsistent with the life you desire, you have an opportunity to do something new this year!

If you are facing a reality that suggests something new is needed, know that you have many opportunities to do something new. Areas to consider are your:
- Philosophy
- Practices
- Beliefs
- Mindset
- Approaches
- Pace
- Commitment
- Partnerships
- Planning
- Process
- Strategy
- Priorities
- Focus
- Problem solving
- Perseverance
- Ability to receive feedback
- Learning
- Time management
- Communication

You might also consider tackling a particular area of your life like:
- Finances
- Relationships
- Health

Once you have identified an area, begin by dedicating time to it and monitoring what happens when you do it. This will allow you to determine if your new efforts are yielding the results you desire.

Be aware! You may experience difficulty or discomfort, as you try something new. This is the nature of growth. The work of growing is called *"growing pains"* for a reason. Growth is often accompanied by negative emotions like:
- Dissonance
- Anxiety
- Uncertainty
- Grief
- Fear

While uncomfortable, these emotions are not indicative of the value of trying something new. They are merely an indication that you are growing in a new way. You experience dissonance when your new life or choices are inconsistent with what you have known to be true. Maybe you told yourself that nothing is possible and then you discovered through your new choices that many more things are possible.

You experience anxiety and uncertainty when you are trying new things because you have never experienced the results of your new choices. Moreover, it can be common to experience grief when trying something new because you are losing your old practices and outcomes as well as the certainty or stability that came with them no matter how deleterious they were. Don't be deterred. Losing bad results for better results is good! Lastly, if you try something new and it does not result in the impact you desire, do not be discouraged. Try something new until you find the thing for you!

Connect With Tiffany

www.sherisesstudios.com/tiffanytyler
www.drtylerinspires.com
Instagram: #drtgtyler
Facebook: #drtgtyler
TikTok: @blessed.doctor
www.linkedin.com/in/dr-tiffany-tyler-garner-a603431b

STEPPING OUT OF THE UNIFORM TO FIND FREEDOM

By **Abbie Westgate**

It was the moment I'd been waiting for - the day I finally got to deliver my bespoke, trauma informed wellbeing training to my former colleagues. It's what I'd created Healing Blue Hearts to do. But instead of feeling proud, my inner voice was screaming at me *'this isn't it!'*.

The attendees themselves were great, but I could tell my work wasn't landing the way I'd truly hoped. I knew some of this was down to cultural and environmental factors within the police itself, but I also realised there needed to be a readiness within the individual too.

Whilst it was empowering to see who I'd become on the other side of a system that left little room for vulnerability or emotional expression, I knew that the fight to make any meaningful change would be constant.

And I didn't want to fight anymore.

So I made the decision to close Healing Blue Hearts, which left me feeling like a failure. And in letting go of my business, I was letting go of the last connection to my former life, so there was a grief in that too.

But I also felt a huge sense of relief, and that's how I knew I'd made the right choice. Just when I thought my work with surrender was done (haha), I found myself even deeper than before - no career, no business, no direction.

Once again I was faced with the unknown, and allowed it to become my teacher. Not that I had much choice - it was like being placed in a waiting room, knowing only that you're going to be there a while!

This time I didn't resist, I let go - a full on trust fall into the dark where I expected to hit rock bottom... only it never came. Here I was, living my biggest fear, and instead of collapse, there was freedom.

With nowhere to go, and nobody to be, life took on a spaciousness that afforded me this deep, restorative rest. I had nothing left but my story, and I took this as a sign that it was ready to be witnessed.

It was like time had stood still for this moment and life was holding its breath, as I poured the truth of the last few years into the pages of my book.

For me, writing a memoir has felt like soul work, and I'd never have touched these depths had I not learned to honour the seasons of life.

In the same breath, I'm not here to romanticise the challenges of my journey - I have a much lower income, I've lost confidence, I worry about the future, and most days I feel I'm walking this path completely alone.

Then there's the comparison trap that comes with seeing others around you doing great things, whilst your life feels very much on hold. This often tiggers an urge to chase the external, but I've learned this is just fear trying to force or speed things up to create certainty.

So you see, surrender in this form is far from passive. It's a hard-earned state of being that asks for groundedness, awareness and trust. Not always easy when life is testing your limits, but the ability to self-resource creates an inner wealth that transcends financial status.

And yes, allowing myself to be seen this way feels vulnerable, but if the alternative is to only feel worthy when I have achievements to share, then I'd rather stand for inner beauty, strength and truth.

I'm a fitness coach, a breathwork teacher, and I'm writing a book.

And for now, that's enough.

Connect With Abbie

Instagram: @abbiewestgate_breathwork

CRAFTING YOUR BUSINESS IN GOD'S BACKYARD (YES, REALLY)

By **Andrea C Russell**
Business Implementation & Financial Accountability Coach

Let me guess.

You thought stepping into entrepreneurship would feel like crossing into the Promised Land milk, honey, and consistent Stripe notifications, right?

Instead, you got a divine detour, a mountain of self-doubt, and a budget that makes ramen look luxurious.

Welcome to the club.

This isn't your average business success story. I didn't launch from a co-working space with coconut lattes and Pinterest-worthy planners. I launched from my prayer closet. Broke. Bold. Barely breathing. But God? He was already building something in his backyard while I was still crying in mine.

From Brokenness to Boardrooms

Before I ever collected a client, I collected pain. Church hurt. Financial mess. Single motherhood. And a degree in trying to do it all while pretending I had it all together.

Let me be real: I didn't start a business because I was brave. I started one because God told me to and I was too scared *not* to obey.

The *"aha moment"* came somewhere between a crisis of faith and a call from a stranger who found my website and paid me in full. No ad, no pitch, no funnel. Just, favor.

That's when I realized: I wasn't building a business. I was answering a *Kingdom* call.

Business Is Holy Ground

Most of us grew up hearing money is evil, sales are manipulative, and good Christian women don't chase profit, they wait for manna.

Let me go ahead and break that lie in half.

Profit isn't the problem. Poverty mindset is. And Scripture? It never told you to stay broke to prove your faith.

In Her Path to Entrepreneurship Anthology, my chapter *From Prayer to Profit: Crafting Your Business in God's Backyard* shares exactly how I flipped the script, not just in my mindset, but in my methods.

Spoiler alert: It starts with prayer.

But it ends with *profit on purpose*.

My Method Is Messy and It Works

No fluff, no formulas. Just a framework I call S.O.A.R.
- Surrender to God's plan
- Overcome obstacles (especially the ones in your head)
- Align your actions with His Word
- Rise up and walk in purpose

This is the same process I walk through in the *Prayer to Profit Workbook*. It's not a *"manifest it"* vibe. It's *"get on your knees, then get in position."* Because favor falls on action not anxiety.

Faith + Strategy = Unstoppable

This is for the woman who's tired of asking for permission to prosper. The one who's scared to raise her prices because the church lady in her head keeps whispering, *"Who do you think you are?"*

Here's your answer: You are called. You are capable. You are already on God's VIP list.

You don't need another webinar. You need a workbook that holds your hand while pointing you straight to the Throne.

Final Truth Here

Business doesn't have to break you.

You can build from a broken place, led by peace not pressure, faith not force. My story didn't start with a strategy, it started with surrender.

So if you've been wondering if God can use *your* story to build something beautiful, let me answer that with every fiber of my being:
Yes, He can. Yes, He will. And yes, it might just start in the backyard.

Want to S.O.A.R. in your business with supernatural favor and God-sized confidence? Grab my chapter in *Her Path to Entrepreneurship* and let the *Prayer to Profit Workbook* become your new secret weapon.

Because baby girl, it's your time to build with boldness, with faith, and yes, with profit.

Grab your copies here
https://businesscoach.andrearussellcoach.com/home

Connect With Andrea

www.businesscoach.andrearussellcoach.com/home
www.amazon.com/author/andreacrussell
Instagram: Christianwomenpreneur
www.facebook.com/groups/christianwomenprenuer

SHE RISES STUDIOS

Live Tour

10 CITIES. 2 WEEKS. EMPOWERING WOMEN EVERYWHERE.

JANUARY 12-26   REGISTER NOW

OFFICIAL COLLABORATOR

EMPOWERHER CONTENT DAY 02 | 22 | 2026 ALLEGIANT STADIUM – LAS VEGAS

EMPOWERHER
POWER PARTNER PROGRAM

Join a global movement inside Allegiant Stadium and be recognized as a driving force behind one of the most powerful empowerment events in history.

APPLY TO BECOME A POWER PARTNER

By **Marion King**

Every day begins with a quiet return to myself. Before emails, painting, or plans, I turn to a few small practices that help me stay grounded. A gratitude walk, three handwritten pages, and a few minutes of stillness. These simple rituals care for my inner world, and create a steady foundation beneath everything else. Over time they've shown me that being *"unstoppable"* doesn't come from constantly striving, but from listening inwards and staying connected to what feels true inside.

Each morning begins in that quiet, silvered light before the world fully wakes. I step outside and begin my gratitude walk, twenty-five unhurried minutes to listen, to notice, and to remember what it feels like to be alive. The birds are calling to one another, the earth is cool beneath my feet, and the air carries the scent of something new. I notice the small things, fallen leaves, a single feather, tiny flowers pushing through the grass, and the shadows of palm fronds dancing across the white garden walls.

As I walk, I name the things I am grateful for. Some are outer blessings, the people I love, the home that holds me, and the food that nourishes me. Others are quieter, unfolding within, patience, resilience, moments of peace. Gratitude gathers itself gently when I move like this, step by step, thought by thought, until everything feels connected.

When I return, I write. Three pages longhand, a practice inspired by *The Artist's Way* by Julia Cameron. It is a conversation with myself that no one else will ever read. I begin with the day before, small details, half-formed thoughts, and questions that have followed me into the morning. I write until my mind begins to clear, until the noise inside becomes softer. It is less about crafting sentences and more about letting go, releasing what no longer needs to be held.

Later, I meditate. This is where stillness becomes luminous. I begin by connecting to source, drawing pure platinum light from high in the universe. I imagine it flowing through my crown, spiralling down through my body. The light extending like radiant roots, reaching deep into the crystalline heart of the earth. When it rises again, it weaves heaven and earth within me, a single healing energy of peace and presence.

These three practices of walking, writing, and stillness have become my way home. They remind me that self-care is not something we add to our lives, it is how we return to ourselves. In the quiet spaces of reflection, we begin to remember our own light and the calm strength that was never lost.

As the new year begins, I find myself moving with gentler intention, noticing what feels nourishing, and allowing space for what wants to grow. Renewal isn't a rush or a resolution. It's a soft unfolding from within.

What does it mean to be unstoppable? For me, being unstoppable is how we keep showing up for life, not perfectly but with heart. It's the courage to rest rather than push, to listen when our hearts whisper, and to begin again, softly, when we're ready.

Strength doesn't always need to be loud. Often it's gentle, steady, deeply human.

Self-care for the soul isn't about adding more to our to-do lists, it's about deepening our relationship with the present moment. Through gratitude, honest reflection, and stillness, we can uncover what's always been there; a calm, creative power that guides us forward.

And that, to me, is the essence of being unstoppable.

Connect With Marion

www.marionkingart.com
www.instagram.com/marionkingart
www.pinterest.com/marionkingart
www.linkedin.com/in/marionkingart

A DECISION THAT MADE ME UNSTOPPABLE:
AUGUST 25TH, 2025 (THE ACCIDENT)

By **Dr. Gabrielle T. Booker**

When we imagine transformation, we often picture a dramatic moment—an unmistakable turning point that forever reshapes the way we move through the world. But sometimes, the decision that makes a woman unstoppable begins in a place no one would ever expect.

Most people wouldn't think an accident that should have ended their life could become the catalyst that makes them unstoppable. But in my case, it did. What should have been a critical, devastating moment actually awakened something inside me that had been dormant for far too long.

Before the accident, I lived almost entirely for others.

I was the woman who said yes even when it drained me, who showed up even when I was breaking, who gave and gave—even at the expense of my own safety, well-being, and happiness. Ninety-nine percent of the time, I put myself last because I believed approval was the currency of love. I thought that being needed was the same as being valued.

But the accident forced me into a truth I had avoided for years:
When you live for everyone else, you eventually disappear from your own life.

The Awakening

Lying there, confronted with the fragility of everything I had taken for granted, something shifted. The version of me who always sought validation—who chased love, acceptance, and belonging—finally exhaled. And in that quiet, something new rose.

I realized that sometimes the bravest thing a woman can do is simply survive.
That some days, being proud of myself for breathing was enough.
That existing—fully, unapologetically, and in my truth—was already a miracle.

The accident awakened the little girl in me who had always wanted to be loved, to be seen, to be understood. She had spent years molding herself into what others needed, hoping someone would finally say, You matter. You're enough.

But instead of waiting for someone else to give her that validation, I finally decided to give it to myself.

The Decision That Changed Everything

With that new awareness came a decision—one that still reverberates through every part of my life:
I will no longer abandon myself for the comfort, approval, or expectations of others.

I began choosing myself with intention and courage:
- Setting boundaries I once feared.
- Honoring my needs without apology.
- Letting my voice hold the same weight as everyone else's.
- Celebrating the small wins and the quiet triumphs.

Standing tall in the truth that I am worthy—not because of what I give, but because of who I am.

It was not a loud transformation, but a steady one. Each step toward self-respect became a step toward freedom. Each moment of self-recognition became an act of healing.

I understood, finally, that being unstoppable doesn't mean being unbreakable.
It means refusing to let the breaking define you.

My accident didn't just change my life—it returned me to myself. It awakened a strength I didn't know I had and reminded me that survival is a form of power. It taught me that I don't need permission to take up space, to rest, to speak, to dream, or to become everything I once believed was out of reach.

I became unstoppable the day I realized that my worth was never tied to someone else's recognition—it was something I carried inside me all along.

And if you are reading this, wondering when your own moment will arrive, let this be the reminder you need:
Sometimes the moment that tries to break you is the very moment that awakens the unstoppable woman within you.

Closing Affirmation: Reborn and Unstoppable

From the moment I survived what was meant to break me, I was reborn.

I rise today with the strength of every lesson, the courage of every scar, and the fire of the woman I was always meant to become. I honor my survival, I embrace my healing, and I step forward unshakably whole. My rebirth is my power—and because of it, I am truly unstoppable

Connect With Dr. Gabrielle

Facebook: DrGabrielle Thomas-Booker
Instagram: cmalegacymentoringprogram

THE ULTIMATE SUPERFOOD FOR DOGS

SUPPORTS JOINT HEALTH FOR DOGS OF ALL AGES

Fortified with Vet-Recommended servings of glucosamine and chondroitin

NATURALLY RICH IN COLLAGEN

And infused with Omegas 3, 6, and 9 for Skin & Coat Health

FLAVOR BOOST FOR MEALS

Boosts flavor at mealtime - just a splash over meals has even the pickiest pups licking their bowls clean.

AIDS IN DIGESTION

Supports natural detoxification of the gut and is gentle on sensitive stomachs.

BRUTUSBROTH.COM

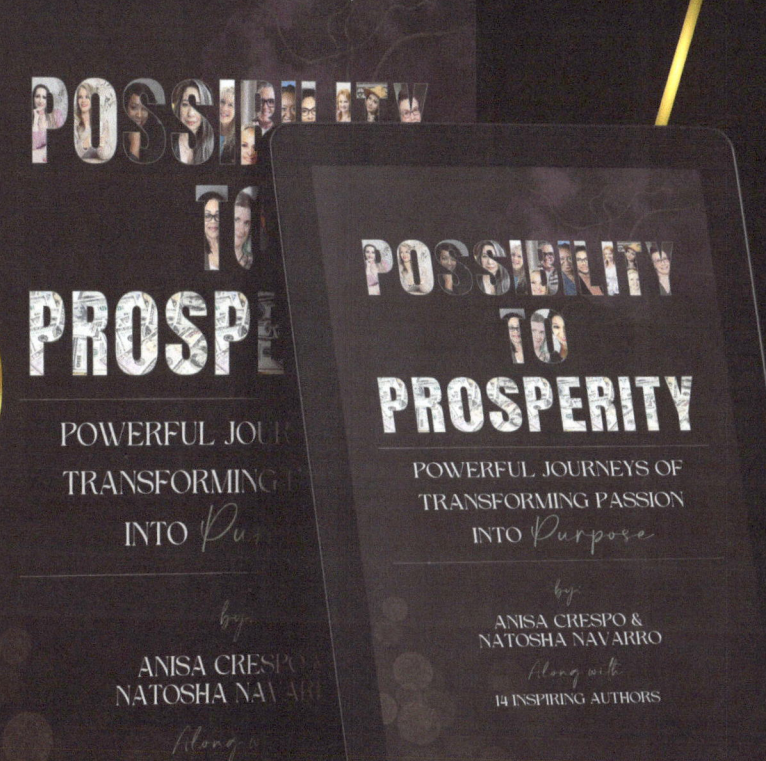

GRAB YOUR COPY NOW

Possibility to Prosperity is an inspiring anthology featuring bold, visionary women who turned their greatest struggles into triumphs. Through honest and powerful stories, these women reveal how pain can become purpose, fear can become fuel, and setbacks can spark success. From heartbreak and burnout to rejection and failure, each chapter offers lessons in resilience, reinvention, and reclaiming one's worth. With courage and determination, these stories illuminate the path from challenge to opportunity, showing that it's never too late to rise, build, and thrive. This book reminds every reader that your struggles can be the gateway to your greatest possibilities.

amazon.com   **SHE RISES STUDIOS**

THE WEDDING I LOST, THE LIFE I FOUND

By **Sam Friedrich**

When my 2020 wedding was canceled during Covid, I did not realize that the box of sola wood flowers I had already purchased would end up redirecting the course of my life. At the time, I was simply trying to create something meaningful from a moment that felt completely upended. I started painting the flowers, partly to distract myself and partly to salvage a small part of what I had imagined my wedding day would look like. What I did not expect was how much joy I would find in the process. The quiet focus of painting each petal and the satisfaction of shaping a bouquet became a source of calm I had not known I needed.

I began making bouquets for friends and family, then small pieces for their homes. Each gift felt like a way to share something hopeful during a difficult year. People soon began asking if they could commission their own pieces. It was never meant to be the beginning of a business. It was simply something I loved doing and something that made other people feel seen and celebrated.

At the time, I was working in a corporate program management role. On nights and weekends, I was building a small creative practice without consciously planning it. I took custom orders when I could and slowly developed a style that felt like mine. The work grounded me in a way my corporate life never had. Even on stressful days, sitting down to paint flowers created a sense of steadiness I could not find anywhere else.

In October of this year, I was laid off from my corporate job. For a moment, it felt like another major disruption, much like the canceled wedding. But this time I recognized something familiar in the uncertainty. Life had gone off script before, and something unexpectedly good had come from it. I had already spent years building this craft in the margins of my day. Choosing to step into it full time did not feel reckless. It felt earned.

Today, my designs live at *SolaFlowerSam.com*, where I create wedding florals, custom gifts, and home decor for clients across the country. The irony is not lost on me. Losing my own wedding plans is what led me to play a small part in bringing someone else's wedding dreams to life. Every time I pack a bridal bouquet, I think about the moment someone will unbox it. I think about how it might feel to hold something made entirely by hand, knowing it will be carried down an aisle. It is a privilege I never expected to have.

One of the biggest myths about having it all is the belief that life will stay on track if you plan carefully enough. My experience has been very different. The moments that interrupt your rhythm are often the ones that reveal what you are meant to build.

The canceled wedding showed me the joy of working with my hands. The layoff showed me that the foundation I had been building quietly for years was strong enough to stand on.

When challenges appear again, I return to the process that started everything. Painting and shaping each flower gives me momentum I trust. It reminds me that growth often comes from small, steady decisions rather than dramatic breakthroughs. I also keep notes on the turning points I have already faced. Seeing those moments written down reminds me that resilience is not something that arrives all at once. It is something you practice.

What began as a disrupted wedding became a business I love. What looked like an ending in my corporate life became an opening. Every bouquet, every centerpiece, and every hand painted flower is connected to that first unexpected twist. Because of that, I have learned to trust that even the most uncertain moments can lead to something beautiful.

Connect With Sam

www.solaflowersam.com

DOTTIE ROSE
FOUNDATION®

Our mission is to set the standard in computer science education while bridging the gender gap in the technology field.

We envision a future where computer science education is accessible, inclusive, and equitable for all, regardless of gender and a technology industry that values and benefits from the diverse perspectives and contributions of women.

Located Charlotte, NC | **Serving** North Carolina • South Carolina • Floridia • International

LEARN MORE I DOTTIEROSEFOUNDATION.ORG

© A CONTAGIOUS SMILE MEDIA TEAM

SHE TOOK MY HAND IN THE OPERATING ROOM AND I HAVE NEVER FORGOTTEN IT

By **Victoria Cuore**

Some people walk into our lives and quietly change everything. They do not enter with noise or attention. They appear when our hearts are fragile, and our strength feels thin. They bring calm where fear once lived and light into the dark corners we thought would never see it again. Nearly ten years ago, I met one of those rare people. Her name is Dr. McKenzie-Brown, and she redefined compassion.

Living Behind a Guarded Stillness

Before meeting her, I had lived through years of pain, surgeries, and heartbreak. My body had become a map of survival. My daughter had faced even more. Hospitals felt like battlefields. I entered each one prepared for indifference, bracing for disappointment. I had learned that it was safer to expect coldness than to hope for kindness. That guarded stillness became my armor.

A Moment of True Understanding

Then, in a quiet pre-op room, Dr. McKenzie-Brown walked in, and everything shifted. She introduced herself softly, and peace followed her. She met my daughter and instantly seemed to understand our entire story. She saw without me needing to explain. When I told her why I refused sedation and pain medication, she listened without judgment. She honored my choices instead of challenging them. Her respect was quiet but powerful. For the first time in years, I felt truly seen.

A Grounding Presence in the Operating Room

From the moment she entered, her calm strength steadied me. In the bright, cold operating room, fear began to rise again, not for myself but for my daughter. Then she appeared beside me. She reached for my hand, her touch steady and sure. She leaned close and said, *"I have you."* Those three words carried more safety than any promise I had ever heard.

Something inside me released. Then she asked, softly, *"If you could go anywhere right now, where would you want to go?"* She was not distracting me. She was anchoring me, giving me back control in a place where most people lose it.

A Place of Peace Amid Vulnerability

As I answered her, a wave of peace replaced the fear. For a moment, I was not surrounded by machines or strangers. I was free. She reminded me that even when the body is weak, the mind can rest in peace. What she gave me went far beyond medicine. It was healing of the soul.

Consistent Presence and Deep Humanity

Years have passed, and Dr. McKenzie-Brown has never faded from my life. She continues to show up with the same grace and sincerity. She remembers my daughter's name, my fears, and even the smallest details others overlook. She treats me as a person, not a patient. Her care has never been rehearsed or mechanical. It is genuine. It is human.

A Defining Act of Compassion

One day, my daughter needed another surgery at a different hospital. Dr. McKenzie-Brown was not assigned to the case. She had no obligation to be there. Yet she came anyway. She walked into the pre-op room unannounced and wrapped us both in a hug that said more than words ever could. She spoke with the attending physician, offering reassurance that eased my fear. She gained nothing from that visit. She came because she cared. That single act defined her forever.

The Depth of True Presence

She gave me presence when I was breaking. When I could hardly breathe, she gave me steadiness. Her strength became my anchor. Her kindness gave me courage I did not know I still had. She became the stillness in the storm, the reminder that one person's humanity can change how another survives.

A Lasting Appreciation

My gratitude for her runs deep. It lives in every moment she steps in without being asked. It lives in the peace she brought to chaos and the trust she rebuilt in me. She is part of my story now, not because of her title but because of her heart. What she gave my daughter and me cannot be measured. It is a love rooted in respect and understanding.

Enduring Impact

Every time I walk into a hospital now, I carry her with me. Her influence lives in the way I breathe through fear and the way I believe that goodness still exists. I no longer feel powerless when I step into those rooms. I carry a calm that began the day she placed her hand over mine and whispered, *"I have you."*

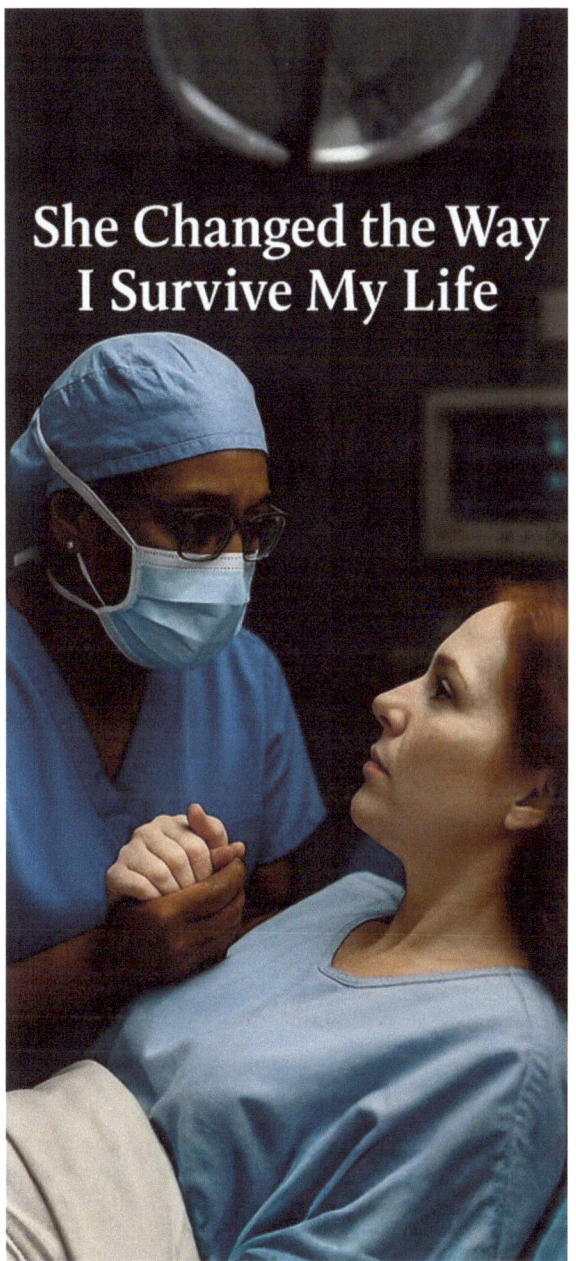

That moment did not just change how I faced surgery. It changed how I face life. She not only helped me heal. She reminded me that I am still whole.

Connect With Victoria

www.acontagioussmile.mn.co
www.facebook.com/profile.php?id=61576680343801
www.instagram.com/acontagioussmile1
Podcast: A Contagious Smile — available on all major platforms

CHAOS & CAFFEINE:
THE GLOBAL ADDICTION TO BURNOUT

By **Dr. Cali Estes**

Across every continent, there is a familiar sound at dawn, the whir of coffee machines. Mugs are lifted like armor before the battle of the day begins.

From bustling Nairobi cafés to fluorescent boardrooms in New York, caffeine has become the socially acceptable drug of high performers.

It fuels ambition, masks exhaustion, and disguises emotional depletion. Yet beneath the foam and sugar rush lies a growing crisis of global burnout, a quiet pandemic eroding mental health, relationships, and purpose.

As someone who has coached CEOs, professional athletes, and entertainers for more than twenty-five years, I have witnessed this addiction firsthand.

We do not call it *"addiction,"* because it comes wrapped in productivity. But caffeine, sugar, and chaos have become coping mechanisms for unprocessed stress and overstimulated nervous systems. We sip our anxiety instead of healing it.

Modern life rewards speed, not stillness:
Notifications, deadlines, and constant connectivity flood our brains with dopamine spikes that mimic the highs of substance use.

The body responds; adrenaline surges, cortisol rises, and sleep declines.

When exhaustion hits, we reach for another espresso to push through. The pattern repeats until "tired but wired" becomes the new normal.

According to the World Health Organization (WHO), burnout is now an occupational phenomenon affecting hundreds of millions worldwide.

The International Labour Organization estimates that stress-related illnesses cost the global economy more than one trillion dollars each year in lost productivity.

Yet instead of addressing the root causes such as toxic work cultures, unrealistic expectations, and emotional isolation, we double down on quick fixes. Caffeine and chaos are not the problem; our dependency on them is. They have become substitutes for self-worth and momentum. For many professionals, the latte in hand is less about taste and more about identity: proof they are still producing.

The most successful people are often the most vulnerable. Executives, founders, and high-achievers are trained to tolerate discomfort and *"push through."*

But that drive can mutate into self-neglect. In my work, I see a recurring theme: professionals hiding exhaustion behind performance.

They are the ones who say, *"I am fine, I just need another coffee."* They joke about being "addicted to chaos," yet their nervous systems are in constant fight-or-flight. They chase the next launch, the next deal, the next high, until their bodies finally revolt.

It is not just burnout. It is emotional addiction.

The brain becomes conditioned to seek adrenaline and to equate peace with boredom. This is why a silent weekend feels unbearable and why checking emails at midnight feels strangely satisfying. We are wired to crave the chaos we claim to hate.

Caffeine is the world's most consumed psychoactive substance.

It sharpens focus temporarily but, when overused, elevates cortisol, the stress hormone, and disrupts natural sleep cycles. Paired with refined sugar, it creates the perfect storm: a dopamine rush followed by an emotional crash.

Societies have normalized this biochemical roller coaster as *"hustle culture."* We glorify exhaustion as evidence of dedication and reward overextension with promotions. But the cost is immense: anxiety, depression, chronic fatigue, and decreased empathy. The United Nations Sustainable Development Goal 3, Good Health and Well-Being, calls for global attention to mental health as essential to sustainable societies. True productivity can no longer be measured by output alone. It must include emotional stability, creativity, and connection, traits that thrive only in a regulated nervous system.

The Chaos and Caffeine Mindset Shift

Breaking free begins with awareness. When I teach executives and creatives how to *"biohack burnout,"* I do not tell them to quit coffee; I teach them to quit chaos. Five small shifts can change everything:

- **Pause Before You Pour:** Ask, *"Am I tired or just disconnected?"* Often the body needs rest, not stimulation.
- **Replace, Don't Remove:** Swap your third coffee for hydration, breathing, or adaptogens that balance the adrenals.
- **Schedule Silence:** Stillness repairs the nervous system. Protect it like any other meeting.
- **Feed the Brain, Not the Buzz:** Nutrient-dense foods stabilize mood far better than caffeine ever will.

- **Redefine Worth:** Success is not how much you do; it is how deeply you live.

Recovery from chaos is not laziness, it is leadership. When leaders prioritize rest and mental hygiene, they model a new paradigm of performance that values humanity over hustle.

A Final Sip of Sanity

In every corporate keynote I deliver, I ask, *"What if peace, not pressure, was your power source?"*

The room always falls silent. We have forgotten that calm is a skill, one that can be trained.

Healing the burnout epidemic requires more than coffee alternatives. It means re-educating cultures to value rest, resilience, and regulation.

Governments, organizations, and individuals must also work together to dismantle the myth that constant doing equals success. Caffeine may fuel our mornings, but consciousness must fuel our future.

The next time you reach for that second cup, remember that your worth is not measured by exhaustion. The world does not need another over-caffeinated achiever; it needs leaders who are awake in spirit, not just in body.

So breathe. Slow down. Let the coffee cool if it must.

In that quiet moment between sips lies the clarity the world is craving.

Connect With Dr. Cali

www.caliestes.com
www.facebook.com/DrCaliEstesOfficial
www.instagram.com/dr._cali_estes
www.linkedin.com/in/caliestes
www.youtube.com/@CaliEstes

Write the Book That Positions You as the Authority

At She Rises Studios, we don't just publish books.
We help you launch movements, legacies, and platforms for visibility.

This is your moment to claim your place as a founder-author.

✨ Full publishing services included   ✨ You keep 100% rights & royalties   ✨ Visibility across our media ecosystem

ENROLL NOW

POWERED BY

SHE RISES STUDIOS **FENIX TV**

02 | 22 | 2026

EMPOWERHER CONTENT DAY

ALLEGIANT STADIUM – LAS VEGAS

ONE STADIUM. 40,000 WOMEN. INFINITE IMPACT

Q&A WITH USA TODAY BESTSELLING AUTHOR ANN CHARLES

By **Ann Charles**
USA Today Bestselling Author

Q: Where do you find the inspiration for each one of your books including your latest, Time Reaping in Deadwood?

I've always found real life to be stranger than fiction, so I enjoy the everyday tales of life coming from friends, family, strangers in the grocery store checkout line, and posts on social media. I also love to watch movies and series for inspiration. Usually, something I see along the way will spark an idea for an entertaining plot thread within one of my on-going series.

For my latest book, Time Reaping in Deadwood, I had fun learning about tarot reading. I included elements of it as a humorous thread throughout the book that also added to the suspense for what was to come for Violet Parker, the main character in this series.

Q: Is it difficult to combine more than one element when writing a book?

Mixing genres comes naturally for me. In my early days of writing, I tried to stick with mostly one element. First it was romance. Then it was mystery. But I struggled to put it on the page. After I decided to let the story flow and see what came out, I realized that my struggles had been because I'd been trying too hard to fit into one genre. So, I let the story roll out and ended up with a tale that blended several elements and didn't fit easily into one genre. Then I had a new problem—how to sell this mixed-genre story in a world with pre-set, somewhat rigid categories in the publishing industry. Lucky for me, at this time the entertainment industry was changing, and mixed genre movies and stories were starting to become popular. It was then a matter of finding readers who enjoyed the type of elements in my mixed genre stories, which took some time, but that's another story.

Q: Your books are well-known and loved for the humor, action, and adventure packed scenes.

Were you always this talented or did you have to work to get to where your writing is today?

I had to work and work and work, and I'm still trying to improve with every book I write. Over the years, I've studied some of my favorite books, breaking them down into scene and sequel, studying how the transitions were crafted, making notes on body language, analyzing dialogue and character growth. I worked to understand the purpose of themes and premises, figuring out how to better incorporate them into my stories. I experimented with various tropes and plotted out series arcs, keeping in mind how a binge reader would feel as they cruised through not just one story, but multiple books.

One of the struggles with writing a longer series is holding a reader's attention. This is something I study in other long-running series, considering different ways to keep the humor fresh as I move from one book to the next. In order to be successful, I think I have to keep studying and experimenting with new techniques. Not only will this benefit the reader, but it will keep me from growing bored with telling the story.

Q: Who are the main characters in TimeReaping in Deadwood?

Violet Parker is the main and only point-of-view (POV) character in the Deadwood Mystery series, so we only ever see the story unfold through her eyes. This first person technique is nothing new in the publishing world, but for years I only wrote in third person. Violet's series is the first and only where I write from a single POV. There is a challenge in this style of storytelling that I enjoy, and while it can be limiting on some levels, it also can really raise the suspense in a scene. I think telling the story in this way also helps the readers feel like they know Violet better due to a deeper POV.

Other than Violet, there is a cast of secondary characters that includes her quirky friends, her aunt, her kids, and boyfriend. There are some great villains readers love to hate, and some really creepy supernatural characters that add some great scares, too. To help readers keep track of everyone, after the first few books I began including a cast of characters at the front of the books and list in which books the characters star.

Q: What themes will readers find inside of TimeReaping in Deadwood?

There are a lot of tricky devils in this story who give Violet plenty of heartburn, and there is no such thing as coincidence for her and her friends. She's growing stronger mentally in this book, learning when to fight and when to run.

While the last book in the series (Book 12: Never Say Sever in Deadwood) had a lot of physical action, this book follows with more character growth blended with humor. I think it's important with a long series to keep track of how characters are changing in addition to moving the plot and subplots forward book after book.

Q: How many books are in The Deadwood Mystery Series? How many do you plan for the whole series?

Currently, there are 13 books in the series. I'll be working on the 14th book next year, and there will be more books after that. I used to say that I'd write 12 books and see how things were going at that point. Well, 13 books later, the series is still going strong, so onward we go. At this time, I don't have a set number of books for how long this series will last. I'm traveling along a series arc, but I'm allowing the storyteller in my head to move at her own pace. As it is often said, it's all about the journey, not the final destination.

Q: As an indie writer, do you set-up deadlines to complete each one of your books?

There are so many roles as an indie writer that have nothing to do with actually writing the books. For example, I have to spend a significant amount of time promoting each book and coming up with next ways of marketing my stories. I also have to spend time doing bookkeeping every month to stay on top of the financial parts of the business so that I can keep the tax folks happy. There is new software to learn to keep up with the publishing trends, and don't forget all of the time it takes to keep up on social media creating new content. Each book requires energy to market, and continuing to keep my backlist of books selling takes even more brain power. So, if I don't set a deadline to complete a book and push hard to hit that deadline, it is really easy to not write day after day and not create any new content for readers. No new stories means an author is no longer relevant and makes it hard to stay up higher in the rankings because the algorithm on major retailers likes popular books. Whew!

Deadlines are motivating and challenging, especially after I announce when a book will be released to readers. I don't like letting them down.

Q: For those who do not know about the book publishing world, how does one become a USA Today bestselling author?

An author has to actually sell a lot of books to readers in a short time in order to make the list. With all of the books being released every week by so many authors, it's not easy to hit any list these days, especially as an indie author with a limited marketing budget. It is really the readers who have the power to help authors make it onto bestselling lists, and I'm grateful to the fans of my stories and characters who have helped me not only land on this list and other bestselling lists, but also win so many writing awards.

Q: What other books are you currently working on at the moment?

I'm working with my husband, Sam Lucky, on the 5th book in the Deadwood Undertaker series, which is a blend of historical fiction, humor, supernatural, and mystery. We hope to have this book out in early 2024.

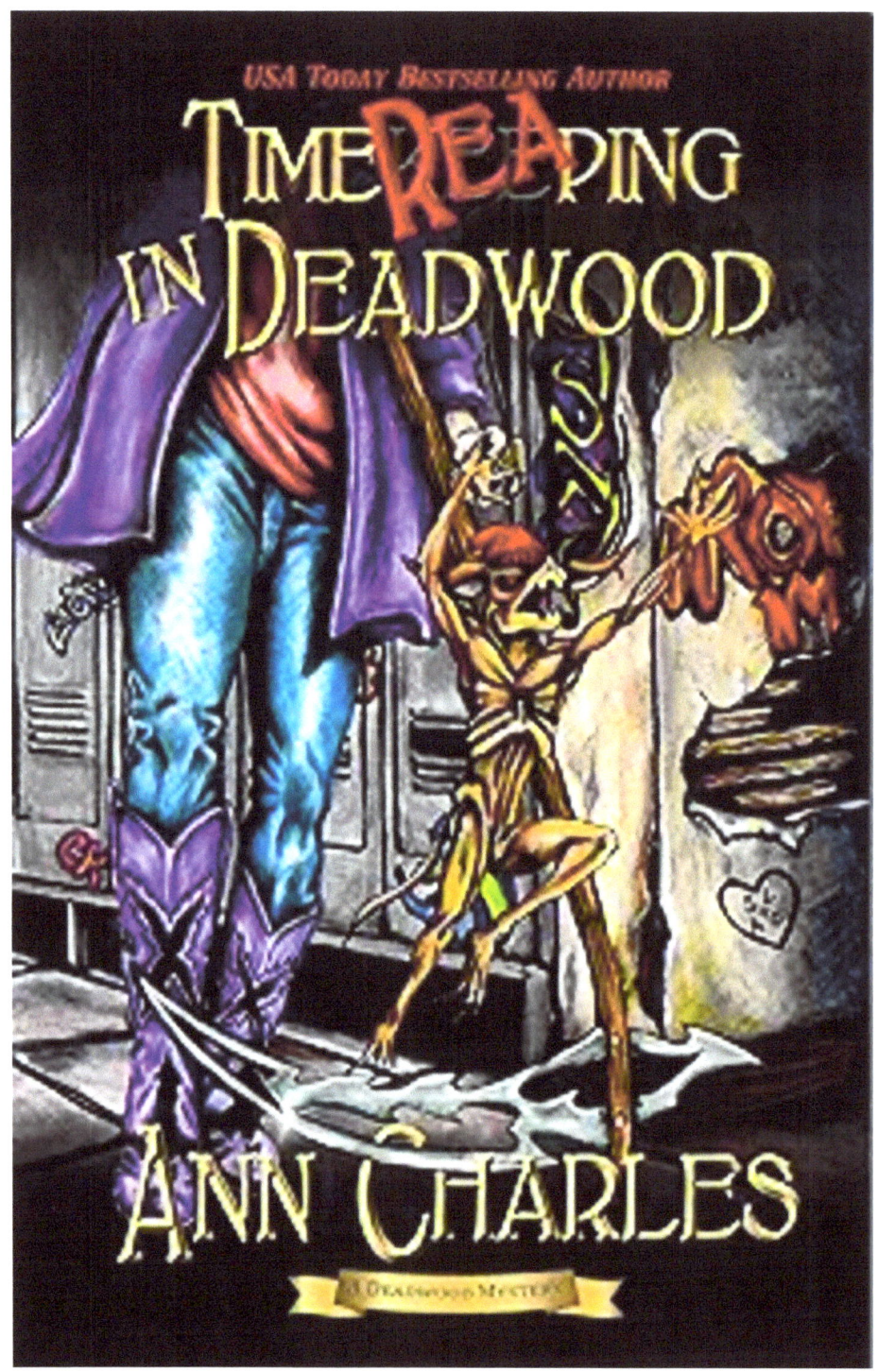

Q: Where can fans find you and your books online?

You can go to my website (*www.AnnCharles.com*) to find links for all my ebooks, print books, and audiobooks on various retailers. You can also find links there to my pages/groups on social media (Facebook, Instagram, LinkedIn, etc.). If you check out the blog section of my website, I have posts that share my past interviews and podcasts, as well as my previous newsletters.

Connect With Ann

www.anncharles.com
www.facebook.com/AnnCharlesAuthorPage
www.x.com/AnnWCharles
www.instagram.com/Ann_Charles

Non-Alcoholic Cocktails

SHOP NOW | DRINKTILDEN.COM

STRUGGLE DEFINES MY SUCCESS

By **Michele Jennae**

What happens when you realize that most of your struggles in life you have brought upon yourself. That's what happened to me! I never planned to fail, but I most definitely failed to plan.

Not for want of trying. I read the books and attended the seminars. And truth be told, I made great strides, accomplishing things that status-quo thinking says is nigh impossible. But something wasn't right in my world.

I had missed the memos to self. I couldn't plan for something I hadn't really defined.

Turning Point

I went back to work in 2024, and it was amazing! Not the job itself – but the fact that the Universe never fails to redeliver an ignored message.

THWACK! The job was awful; the culture was toxic – the most toxic environment I had ever been in. I never thought that a job could cause PTSD until this one.

While I worked there, I showed up every day with words of encouragement for my colleagues. I could see their genius. I also saw their light dimming by the day. Despite the punitive leadership approach and my growing anxiety, I refused to let my spark die. I decided that I could do more outside of this job than in it.

Hello Universe. I hear you. Not even a 25% raise could keep me there. 3 months after the bump in pay, I said, *"No, Thank you. I'm done."* No notice. No safety net. Burn the boats.

Leap of Faith

I decided to reignite my Blue Flame. Come hell or high water I was going to follow the call that had been chasing me my entire adult life. Yes, my Blue Flame was following me. Like any good courtship, it wanted to be chased too!

I decided to rebrand and relaunch, for better or worse, one last time. This time for keeps.

My Blue Flame is inspiring and motivating people to live their best lives, through speaking, writing, and coaching. How could I do that if I wasn't living my best life? No wonder I had been so miserable.

I had to find a way through my challenges – old, unreliable copper cable with no upgrade insight; the nearest networking hotspot almost an hour away; a market seemingly closed to my spiritual and holistic approach to personal transformation.

I got Starlink. I committed to the best and nearest Chamber of Commerce and became an ambassador. I began finding my people.

Challenges are Guaranteed

Nobody said it would be easy. If it were easy, no one would need my coaching! If it was easy, it'd be as useful as doomscrolling Facebook, or eating chocolate bon bons instead of preparing nutritious food, or waiting to win the lottery, usually without ever buying the ticket. Wishful thinking and pipe dreams.

We weren't born for easy. Easy is boring and uninspiring, and honestly a death knell.

Challenges aren't just guaranteed. There's no charge. They just show up and do their thing. Like an employee you can't fire.

The best way to deal with challenges is to 1. Expect them, and 2. Redefine them. It is my goal to be shaped by challenges, embrace them even, as part of the journey. At the end of the day, I will become who I am, more because of how I handled challenges than because of an easy road.

Can I have it all?

Yes, and no. I don't want *"it all"* but I can have all I want when I consider that what I really want is love, growth, accomplishment, and belonging. They are mine for the receiving!

Connect With Michele

www.edgbrio.com
www.Facebook.com/attheEDG
www.instagram.com/michelejennae

WHEN SUCCESS STOPS FEELING LIKE SUCCESS:
THE REBUILD OF A LEADER

By **Emily Aarons**

There's a moment in every conscious leader's journey where the strategy stops working — not because the strategy is broken, but because we are.

I hit that moment hard. From the outside, I was *"living the dream."*

Scaling fast.

Money flowing.

Team expanding.

Metrics soaring.

People applauding.

And yet, I woke up one morning and hated the life I worked so hard to build. Not because I wasn't grateful — I was. But because I was exhausted, overstimulated, suffocating under responsibilities, and quietly asking myself: *"Is this really what I sacrificed so much for?"*

I didn't feel like a visionary or a leader anymore. I felt like a machine: a never-ending source of output and answers and capacity. Like a worker sprinting on a treadmill with a weighted vest, chasing a finish line that never came. And here's the part people don't talk about:

The shame of having everything you thought you wanted and still feeling empty.
The quiet fear that if you slow down, everything will collapse.
The guilt of thinking, *"I don't even want this anymore"* after you fought so hard to build it.
The whisper: *"Who am I if I'm not constantly achieving?"*

We don't say these things out loud because we're afraid we'll lose credibility, clients, respect. We fear people will assume we don't deserve what we've created.

But here's the truth I had to face: Working harder isn't alignment and being busy isn't success.

I did all the *"right"* things. And they worked. But they worked against me energetically.

I was growing, but I was shrinking inside.
I was successful, but I was sacrificing my wellbeing.
I was serving everyone else, but abandoning myself.

I had to stop pretending that another mindset hack, morning routine tweak, or bigger launch would fix the feeling that something fundamental inside me was being ignored. So I did the thing that made absolutely no logical sense:

I stopped.

I turned it all down and stepped away from the metrics obsession. And when I did? My creativity returned like a tidal wave. My nervous system finally exhaled. Joy bubbled back up. And intuition became loud and clear again.

I stopped performing and started remembering who I am. Because hustle might have gotten me here… but alignment is what will carry me forward. And if you're reading this thinking, *"Holy crap, this is me!"* --please breathe this in with your whole body:

You are not failing. You are awakening.
Your soul is not trying to punish you but trying to bring your home.

4 Energetic Shifts to Lead from Alignment, Not Exhaustion

And if you want to reclaim your power, your peace, and your purpose: start here:

1. **Pause Before You Progress** -- Scaling isn't sacred if it costs you your soul.

Instead of asking, *"How can I do more?"*
Ask: *"What needs to soften, release, or recalibrate first?"*

Try:
A 3-minute pause before diving into your day. Close your eyes, hand on heart, breathe.
Ask: What does my energy need today? Spacious success requires space.

2. **Unsubscribe from Over-Proving**
So many high achievers operate from old patterns:
I must earn worthiness.
I must always be producing.
More is safer.

But alignment isn't found in more — it's found in enough.

Ask yourself: "*If I trusted I was already worthy, what would I stop doing today?*"
Let your energy lead: not your fears.

3. **Honor Your Nervous System Like it's Your CEO**
Your nervous system is the real strategy engine:

Regulated = clear, magnetic, intuitive, creative.
Dysregulated = reactive, exhausted, scattered, pushing.

Practice:
Set *"micro-regulation breaks"* throughout your day
one-minute breath reset
sunlight + stretch break
phone on airplane mode for 15 minutes
grounding touch (hand on chest or belly)

Small shifts create quantum returns.

4. **Choose Alignment Over Approval**
When you stop living to be palatable, impressive, or *"correct,"* you become powerful again.

Say no more than you say yes.
Ask: "*Is this choice aligned with who I am becoming — or who I'm afraid to disappoint?*"

Your future self is calling you forward. Answer yourself: not the algorithm, not the pressure, not the expectations.

You didn't come here to build a business that cages you but to create a life and mission that frees you.

I invite you to adopt these new mantras:

I expand by honoring myself, not abandoning myself.
I grow by aligning, not grinding.
I lead by remembering who I am.

This isn't your breakdown but your breakthrough.

You are rising, not because you're pushing, but because you're finally choosing yourself!

Connect With Emily

www.emilyaarons.com
www.instagram.com/emilyaarons
www.linkedin.com/in/emilyaarons
www.facebook.com/emilyaaronsholistic

By **Ana B Castano**
Book author/ International Architect

As the year folds into its final pages, there's a quiet invitation that whispers between the noise and the rhythm of inner listening-of watching the unseen currents that shapes our outer world. Reflection, to me, is not a yearly ritual; it is the pulse of living in awareness. It is how I stay in dialogue with life itself-through silence, gratitude, and the gentle courage to feel deeply.

For quite a long time, I am reminded that Reflection and Gratitude are not passing acts of remembering. They are portals-thresholds that allow to transform experience into wisdom. Renewal doesn't come from erasing what was; it comes from honoring what is, from seeing the sacred thread that has always held us even in the unraveling.

Gratitude as Alchemy

Gratitude when lived consciously, becomes a subtle but powerful force of transformation. It refines perception. It shifts energy. It teaches us to recognize abundance in the invisible-in the breath, in the quiet presence of a friend, in the lessons disguised as loss. I've found that the more I live in Gratitude the more life reveals its order and intelligence.

Each evening, I sit in stillness and give thanks-not only for what was beautiful, but for what stretched me. These moments of acknowledgement soften resistance and make space for clarity. Gratitude doesn't deny pain; it dignifies it. it allows us to say: Even this served my becoming

Reflection as Empowerment

Reflection is a conversation with the soul. It's where truth rises, often softly, beneath the noise. My practice is simple: I journal not to document, but to distill. I ask myself-what did this season show me about trust? Where did I forget my own light? What am I ready to lay down so I can move freely again?

These questions are less about answers and more about attunement. They open inner rooms we often keep closed. In that space of honesty, we remember that growth is not linear-it spirals, it deepens, it returns us home to ourselves.

Renewal through Stillness

Renewal is born in stillness-not in striving, not self-improvement, but in presence. When we become still enough to feel the quiet hum beneath life's surface, we reconnect to source-that place beyond effort, where simply being is enough.

I often begin the day by touching the earth, eyes closed, whispering a simple *thank you (I'm alive and breathing)* That act alone becomes prayer, it reminds me that renewal isn't something that flows naturally when we stop resisting what is.

To close the year consciously is to gather the wisdom of all its moments-the grace and the grit-and to carry forward only what vibrates with truth. Gratitude turns endings into beginnings. It clears the inner field so that what's next can bloom

A Soulful Year-End Practice

As the year turns, create space to sit quietly. Light a candle, breathe, and let your memories unfold without judgement. Write a love letter to yourself-to the woman who kept walking, who kept believing, who kept opening. Thank her for her courage. Then, release what feels heavy. Whisper your intention for the coming year-one word, one wish, one vibration that feels alive in your heart

Connect With Ana

www.anabcastano.com
www.thenomadicdwelling.com
@anabcastano
@anabcastano.author

GRAB YOUR COPY NOW

She Endures: Perseverance Through Pain is a heartfelt anthology honoring women who have faced life's hardest moments and chosen to rise. Through honest, powerful stories of illness, loss, heartbreak, and healing, this collection reveals how pain can shape strength and purpose. Each chapter offers hope, reminding readers that endurance is not just surviving, but growing through what we overcome. Featuring Hanna Olivas, Adriana Luna Carlos, and 11 inspiring authors, this book is a testament to the resilience of women who refuse to give up.

GET YOUR COPY NOW

Celebrate the power of women through inspiring stories and insights.

FAITH, FREEDOM & OTHER F WORDS
RHIANNON ANDERSON

THE ABCS OF SELF-LOVE (JOURNAL)
AMIE RICH

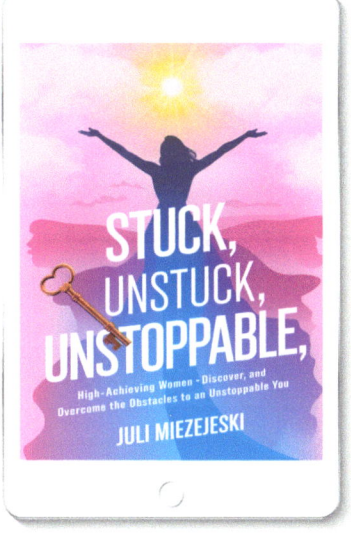

STUCK, UNSTUCK, UNSTOPPABLE
JULIA MIEZEJESKI

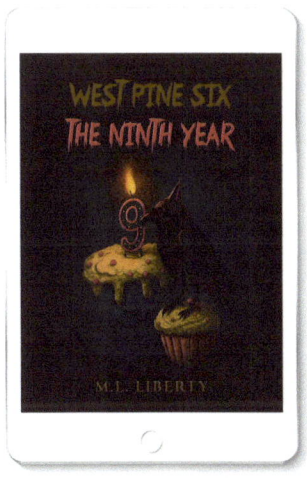

WEST PINE SIX: THE NINTH YEAR
MARIE LAURA LIBERTY

STRETCH & STRETCH JUNIOR
MICHELE KLINE

LIVING BOUNDARIES
GLEN ALEX

 SHOP NOW

PUBLISHED BY
SHE RISES STUDIOS

www.ingramcontent.com/pod-product-compliance
Lightning Source LLC
LaVergne TN
LVHW070438080526
838202LV00035B/2658